REVERSE MORTGAGES

USING YOUR HOME EQUITY TO CREATE A BETTER RETIREMENT

Robert Alfano

Disclaimer

The views expressed in this book are solely the author's and do not reflect the views of any lender or government agency the reverse mortgage is associated with. The information is for educational purposes only and is not meant to be used for any specific tax, legal, or accounting purposes. You should always seek professional advice specific to your needs for those services.

Contents

Foreword

At the time of this writing, I am 61 years old. I wasn't dropped on this planet at 61, and I didn't know anything about reverse mortgages until my 40s. I saw a bunch of really bad TV commercials hawking the loans and lumped them in with payday and title loans, not knowing anything other than the poor marketing I saw. Looking back at the ads, I realize that the companies responsible for them probably did more harm than good by promoting what turns out to be a fantastic program created by Congress to help seniors, much like Social Security and Medicare.

Many people educated me about reverse mortgages, and I want to take a moment to acknowledge some of them. First, there was my Tampa, FL neighbor, Jeremy Shadrick, the founder of the HUD counseling agency, QuickCert. His company counseled 100s of seniors a week about the reverse mortgage product, and it was he who first discussed the loan with me and really made me understand what it was and why it existed.

The next major influence that elevated my education was Marty Aftewicz, my supervisor at AAG. Marty had many years of reverse mortgage experience and was, and remains, a great guy, and I could not have asked for a better mentor than him. His depth of knowledge on the subject and my being placed under his guidance was a stroke of luck for me, and I thank him for his patience and good sense of humor. It is a privilege to call him a friend.

Rob Cooper really gave me a great foundation for understanding reverse mortgages as they relate to buying a home. Matt Neumeyer, founder and President of Premier Reverse Mortgage, is an encyclopedia of all things reverse mortgage and took my knowledge of the reverse mortgage world to a whole other plane of competency.

The academic work of Professor of Finance Jack Guttentag of the Wharton School of the University of Pennsylvania, for decades of research and commitment to the reverse mortgage world. Dr. Wade Pfau, who literally wrote the book on using reverse mortgages for retirement planning, *"Reverse Mortgages: How to Use Reverse Mortgages to Secure Your Retirement."* I consider this book the Bible of reverse mortgages, but be aware that a large part of it is written at a high level for academics and financial professionals! His decades of research and public communication detailing the reverse mortgage product, amongst many other retirement subjects he is an expert on, have helped propel the reverse mortgage conversation in the financial professional community.

Many others helped along the way, but one last big acknowledgment must go out to my wife, Cindy. She has listened to all things reverse mortgage from me, year after year after year after year after year, whether she wanted to or not. Thank you for putting up with me.

1.

Why You Need to Consider Using Your Home Equity

"Every life is organized around a small number of events that either propel us or bring us to a grinding halt. We spend the years between these episodes benefiting or suffering from their consequences until the arrival of the next forceful moment.

A person's worth is established by the number of these defining circumstances we are able to create for ourselves.

We need not always be successful, for there can be great honor and much learning in defeat. But we ought to be the main authority in these decisive scenes of our existence, whether they be epic or tragic.

Whatever the past may have handed you, it is up to each one of us to chisel our future out of the shapeless block that is the present."

\- ***Hernan Diaz.***

When I first read this in the Pulitzer-winning novel *"Trust"*, I was really taken aback by how profound and frighteningly accurate this passage is. If you really think about it, there are major events that happen to us throughout our lives, either within our control or by an act of fate, that change us from that moment on. Sometimes these moments are crystal clear, like marriage, birth of a child, death of a family member, and so many other examples that you can look back on with clarity and pinpoint that moment that forever changed you.

Other times, these moments disguise themselves as ordinary days when you make a decision that seems minor, only to look back many years later and realize how significant an impact they had on you. The problem with these moments is that you can't recognize them when they happen.

Retirement decisions mostly fall into the latter group of these benign days. You can't appreciate the impact of your choices made throughout your life until the moment finally arrives when you reach a point where you are ready to reap the rewards of your life's work, and only then can you finally see and evaluate just how good or bad your choices in retirement planning were.

Academics have studied the way we save, and based on decades of research and their findings, they have advised Congress, the Executive branch, and many government agencies that have helped shape national policy for Social Security, Disability, Medicare / Medicaid and many other departments that contribute resources to our health, wealth and access to programs and services for our benefit in retirement.

Unfortunately, the research mostly found that we were making decisions that put us in financial jeopardy by not saving enough. This isn't new. The trend began in the 1980s, when traditional pensions were phased out in favor of 401(k)s and other savings programs, and the average worker became increasingly responsible for their own finances. They started contributing less to their future for various reasons. In the early 21st century, we saw that the savings needed for a comfortable retirement and the savings people actually had were becoming an issue. Their quality of life in retirement was being compromised compared to that of the previous generation.

This problem has only grown with the next generation, so now that we are in 2026, a generation later, all the research shows that we have less to spend on ourselves, when adjusted for inflation, than the generation before.

It is alarming, and we are near a retirement crisis in America, which is why any resource you can access to help you in retirement needs to be reevaluated and considered. This is why the Reverse Mortgage needs to be discussed as a part of your retirement planning. Your home is one of the most underutilized sources of wealth you have, and the Federal government created the Reverse Mortgage to help seniors age in place so they do not need to sell their home to survive after they have depleted their savings.

This book will explain why the Reverse Mortgage exists, why it is structured the way it is, and the many ways you can use your home wealth to your advantage and still leave a financial legacy to your heirs.

Why Was the HECM Created?

Let's start from the beginning.

The creation of the Home Equity Conversion Mortgage (HECM), the legal name for the FHA-insured reverse mortgage, was not by accident. In 1969, PhD Yung-Ping Chen from the University of Massachusetts began researching how to improve the Social Security program and what else seniors could access to help them in retirement. Dr. Chen was a professor of Economics and Gerontology, the study of the biological, cognitive, cultural, psychological, and social aspects of aging. He served as a delegate to four White House conferences on aging from 1971 to 2005. His work helped legislators improve Social Security, and many of his ideas are still implemented today. He also developed innovative ideas to improve long-term care benefits and eventually the HECM.

The idea of the reverse mortgage wasn't new at the time. The first reverse mortgage in the U.S. was in the 1960s, but there were no federal regulations, and they were not streamlined in terms of how they worked or what each one offered. The banks that offered them set the rules.

Since they were not regulated, the terms and conditions were poor, and they were seen as a last resort to prevent someone from getting foreclosed on.

Dr. Chen and many in government saw a bigger issue: many people were becoming more house-rich and income-poor. This prompted them to look more closely at the reverse mortgage concept and whether it could be applied nationwide on a large scale to help homeowners who could benefit from the loan. In 1981, the White House Conference of Aging commissioned a pilot program to create the HECM, and by 1989, the first HECMs were available through the Department of Housing & Urban Development.

HUD's mission statement for reverse mortgages was and still is: "To enable seniors 62 and older to convert home equity into tax-free income, to support aging in place, cover living expenses, and pay for home maintenance without needing to make monthly payments or sell the home."

The reverse mortgage is technically a mortgage, but in functionality, it acts like a retirement account. Its entire existence is dedicated to helping seniors in retirement.

The first rollout of the HECM was sloppy, and the product initially had many flaws. Fortunately, most of these issues were resolved over the years, and today's HECM is very different and much better for consumers than it was originally. We will get into these consumer protections later, but I want to briefly discuss some of the major milestones that plagued HECMs early on.

The reverse mortgage had a spotty history, and many older people today still think about the loan the way it was implemented decades ago, before federal regulations put consumer protections in place. Some of the worst offenders in these loans were large banks and insurance companies, and regulations were put in place specifically to address predatory lending by these institutions.

1961: ***The First Loan:*** Nelson Haynes of Deering Savings & Loan (Portland, ME) created the first reverse mortgage. It was completely non-regulated.

1969: ***Senate Recognition:*** Professor Yung Ping Chen introduced the concept to the Senate Special Committee on Aging.

1980s: ***Federal Involvement:*** In 1983, Congress proposed Federal Housing Administration (FHA) insurance to protect against borrower default. Before this time, it was much more common for these loans to go into foreclosure.

1987-1988: ***The HECM Program:*** Congress passed the Housing and Community Development Act of 1987, establishing the Home Equity Conversion Mortgage (HECM) program to regulate the industry and provide non-recourse protection (meaning borrowers won't owe more than the home is worth). Early reverse mortgages raised significant concerns about the potential for seniors to lose their homes, high costs, and the lack of rights or protections for non-borrowing spouses. Before 2008, if a borrower died, a younger spouse not listed on the loan could be forced to leave or face foreclosure. Initial costs were high, sometimes up to 6% of the home's value.

1990s-2000s: *Expansion & Refinancing:* In 1998, the HECM program became permanent. 2004 introduced HECM refinancing, and 2009 introduced HECM for Purchase.

At this time, MetLife & Genworth Financial were both major insurance and reverse mortgage lenders in the market.

The Housing and Economic Recovery Act of 2008 (HERA) significantly restricted the ability of reverse mortgage lenders to sell insurance products in conjunction with these loans, and vice versa. HERA (Public Law 110-289) amended the Home Equity Conversion Mortgage (HECM) statute to prohibit lenders from requiring a borrower to purchase insurance or other financial products as a condition of getting a reverse mortgage. The law prohibits HECM counselors and lenders from being associated with entities that sell financial or insurance products, guarding against conflicts of interest where a lender might steer a senior into an unsuitable annuity or life insurance policy. Before HERA, it was common for insurance lenders to pressure seniors into using the proceeds from their Home Equity Conversion Mortgage (HECM) to purchase annuities, long-term care insurance, or other investment products, often leaving the senior with no cash or equity.

Bank of America and Wells Fargo were also major players in the U.S. reverse mortgage market. Seeing what happened to the insurance companies, both institutions exited the business in 2011 due, among other reasons, to market volatility and regulatory changes enacted to prevent banks from pressuring seniors by offering reverse mortgages to steer them into purchasing other bank products.

2010s-Present: ***Stricter Regulations:*** Following the 2008 financial crisis, the FHA implemented tighter guidelines (e.g., Financial Assessment) to ensure borrowers can pay taxes and insurance. The market began offering both FHA-insured HECMs and private, non-government *("proprietary")* loans.

Today, reverse mortgages are heavily regulated to protect older Americans (62+) by requiring mandatory counseling and capping fees, serving as a tool for aging in place.

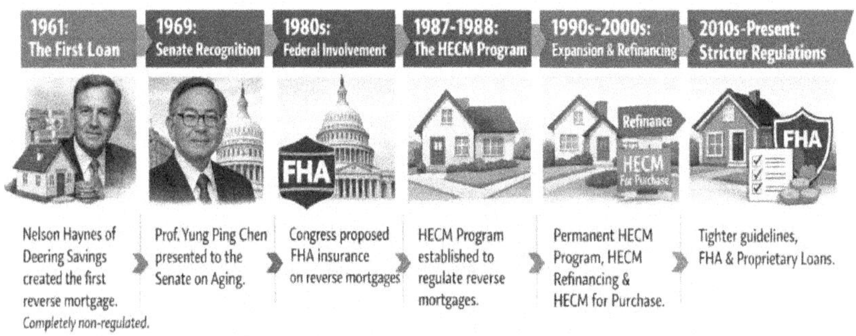

2.

State of the Retirement Nation

Statistically speaking, the single best piece of financial advice is to be born to rich parents in the United States of America. It's an unbeatable advantage. You have to try really hard to fail from this position. If this is not possible, I would offer my second-best piece of advice: become rich parents yourselves or marry into money. I know this sounds jokey and sardonic, and on the surface it is. But it is also profound.

Prioritize choosing a safe place to live with good schools, finding a job with upward mobility built into the company culture, align yourself with other young parents and grandparents who emphasize schoolwork and grades, read books in your home and have conversations about ideas at the dinner table, not just pop culture and gossip, plan sightseeing family trips filled with museums, architecture, history, culture and nature. Save enough money, and you will be set for life.

Sounds so easy, *right?* We all know it isn't, and it is not practical to assume we can all achieve this because statistics tell us we will not. For most of us, we need to plan our retirement carefully and for a very long time, as retirees are living longer than ever before.

Are we as a group really prepared for retirement? In most cases, we are not.

The foundation of a solid retirement portfolio starts with predictable income from Social Security, then, if you are lucky, your pension, investment accounts, and then any other income. Earlier generations largely inherited pensions, but most retirees now do not. Boomers and Gen X now inherit the risk of relying on income in retirement without the safety net of a guaranteed income for life beyond Social Security. Life expectancy is rising, while the promise of a lifetime income isn't. For today's retirees, Social Security isn't supplemental income to pensions like it was years ago; it is a foundation to build on. This means we need other options. Retirement accounts are great if you know you have enough to last your whole life, but if you are not certain, another source of income might be needed.

The single best source of this other income is your home, which we will discuss in detail later. It is the only asset you own that is considered *"non-performing,"* meaning it just sits there doing nothing for you. For most people, it represents a significant unused financial resource and a missed opportunity to tap into their home equity.

The reason you need to be aware of having access to as much cash as possible is the risk of outliving your savings. The image below shows current life expectancy projections for a 65-year-old married couple. A man has a 50% chance of living to 88, while a woman has a 50% chance of living to 90! Beyond this, a man has a 25% chance of living to 94 and a woman to 96.

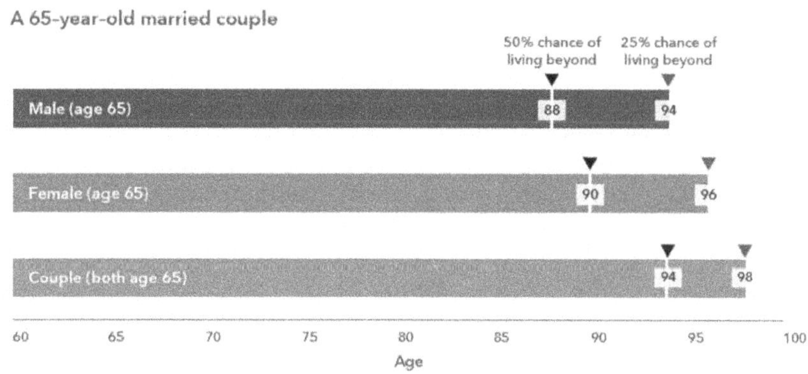

Source: Capital Group and American Academy of Actuaries and Society of Actuaries, as of September 18, 202[illegible]

To compound the issue of having enough money to last, is that in the later years, you will have a substantial need for more cash to help pay for ballooning medical expenses and help around the home, as you will be less likely to physically do many of the routine tasks of keeping up a home that you were able to do years earlier.

You also have to deal with inflation. Historically, SSI does not keep up with the pace of inflation, so you must draw funds from other sources to make up for the increasing costs of living. Inflation runs around 2.25%-2.5% annually, which means that what $1 buys you now would cost about $1.60 to purchase the same item in 20 years.

A recent CNBC article explains why Reverse Mortgages can be so beneficial for so many people. Many who think they may be prepared for retirement find out they are not. Whether it is using a reverse mortgage to help purchase a home to downsize or just opening a line of credit, retaining as much of your savings as possible so they can grow in your retirement is always a good idea.

When discussing my borrowers' finances, I always tell them that if they don't have at least $1 million in their retirement account, a reverse mortgage line of credit should be considered, especially if they have significant medical expenses or plan to travel frequently. If they are purchasing a home and don't have at least $1 million left over after the purchase, then it's the same thing. The $1 million is a rule of thumb, but it works out mathematically most of the time when we calculate savings, expenses, inflation, the death of a spouse, reduced income, health care, and life expectancy.

- In late 2025, 7% of retirees had re-entered the labor force, according to a new AARP survey.
- The two most common reasons people retire are financial readiness or a health issue or disability, according to AARP.
- Of the people who were unretiring, 48% said their primary reason was financial necessity or a poor economic outlook, while 15% cited boredom and 14% said they wanted to stay active, AARP found.

Among those surveyed who are working or looking for work, 41% said their biggest motivation is daily living costs.

We all hope we are prepared for retirement, but we really don't know what the next 20-35 years will look like.

But hope isn't a strategy.

And we all know it.

Hobbies?

Travel?

Vacation Home?

How do you envision your retirement also plays a huge role in how you spend your money? Most people think of retirement spending as a linear, constant event, meaning what you draw from your savings will be predictable each year, but that is not the case. We can adjust how much we take, accounting for inflation, so we may increase the amount we draw from our savings, say, by 3% each year. That is fine, but there is much more to how we spend our money in retirement than that.

Retirement Usually Follows a Three-Phase Pattern for Most Retirees.

Phase 1. It is commonly called the Go-Go Years. You are healthy and maintain an active lifestyle. You socialize in your newfound free time and enjoy many activities and holidays with family, friends, and maybe tour groups on vacation. You tend to want to spend more during this phase, as your health and the health of the people you socialize with are generally very good, and you are capable of doing much of what you want to.

In the Go-Go years, you typically spend more money because you are healthy enough to enjoy doing many of the things you always imagined you would do in retirement. As a result, your portfolio does not grow as much as you think it will, and, in many cases, it is reduced because of all the activity you are doing.

This is perfectly fine, as you worked your whole life and you deserve to enjoy the freedom you now have to pursue the things you put off for so long. The pursuit of happiness is a fundamental right, and it is even enshrined in the Declaration of Independence, which encourages it in society.

- **Phase 2.** Commonly called the Slow-Go Years.

You begin to slow down. Either for health reasons, financial reasons, or changes in your social life, you are not as active or engaged in many of the activities you were earlier in retirement. You start seeing declining health in your social circle and maybe in your own family.

In the Slow-Go years, you typically spend the least amount of money during your retirement. This is due to many factors mentioned above. Your savings have a chance to grow, and you can budget yourself with more discipline than when you were so busy in the earlier part of your retirement.

- **Phase 3.** It Is commonly called the No-Go Years.

You are aging and have now slowed down significantly. Maybe you have declining health, the death of a spouse, or the death of a loved one. You are getting low on financial resources and must budget yourself more strictly than before. You have increased healthcare costs and need more assistance around the home.

In this phase of retirement, you usually wind up spending more money than ever before due to declining health. It is this phase of retirement that most people run through, using up most or all of their savings, and where the anxiety of outliving their portfolio arises. When we are in our early retirement years, we think about this. Still, when the actual crisis occurs, we often must rely on others to help us, either because we are physically or mentally unable to handle many things ourselves.

The Bank of Mom & Dad

As many as half of parents with adult children are stepping in to support their grown kids financially, providing regular assistance for expenses like monthly groceries (83%), cell phones (65%), and even vacations (46%), according to a Savings.com study.

The average amount spent per adult child is at a three-year high of $1,474 per month.

We can't predict when this will happen, but since it is common, we must be prepared if it does. Adult children can drain you financially, and many times it is through no fault of their own.

Covid 19 in 2020-2021 was a perfect example of this. The federal and state governments shut down many businesses, forcing many working people to become unemployed or, if they were business owners, causing their income to fall dramatically for a couple of years.

You see them struggle, and you want to help. This is more painful for you if the grandkids are affected as well. Sometimes, the financial support you offer can mean the difference between a business surviving, the adult child having more time to find a suitable job, and not just some low-paid one that may cause long-term issues, or even keeping the family together, as money problems are the number one cause of divorce.

They may run into serious health issues, or the grandkids may have health issues, and you want to help with the costs until some stability can be managed. There may be an ugly divorce with substantial legal bills or having to give up financial assets.

And sometimes, whether we want to admit it or not, we have an adult child with life issues that force us to make hard decisions about whether to continue supporting them through the latest crises. We hope for the best, but realize that at some point, you can only do so much for them, and that it still affects you emotionally. Emotions can lead you to make irrational financial choices. This is even more so with grandchildren involved.

There is no right answer when it comes to helping family, but that doesn't mean it needs to ruin you financially. You have options.

Financial Emergencies

More Americans are tapping into their retirement savings due to financial emergencies.

In 2025, a record 6% of retirees in 401(k) plans administered by Vanguard Group took a hardship withdrawal. That is up from 4.8% in 2024 and a pre-pandemic average of about 2%, according to Vanguard.

The top reasons for taking hardship withdrawals in 2025 were avoiding foreclosure and eviction, paying medical expenses, and extended family issues, according to Vanguard. The median withdrawal was $1,900.

So, where are retirees financially right now?

The latest Federal Reserve Survey of Consumer Finances reports that the average retirement account for couples aged 65-74 is $609,230. The median savings are even lower than that.

The average pre-retirement income for couples is $125,100.

The standard amount in the Financial Advisor community you need to save for retirement is about 10 times your annual salary. For the average couple, this is around $1.2 million.

This means that, on average, U.S. retirees need to come up with almost twice as much money as they currently have in savings.

BlackRock, the world's largest asset management firm, conducted a 2025 survey of people close to retirement, and the results showed that most people feel they need closer to $2 million to retire comfortably. That may be fear dictating many responses, but it shows how many people think they are not prepared for retirement.

For some, maybe $2 million would be an ideal amount saved for the type of retirement they have planned. For many others, they don't need that much money.

If you take 5% of your savings annually and have $1 million saved, that is $50,000, or just over $4,000 a month. If you pay taxes on any of that, then your net amount is even less. Combine that with SS, and for a couple, maybe your monthly income is double. Can most couples live on $8,000 a month? Sure, they can, but if they want to travel a lot, help fund the grandkids' college, or buy a vacation home, then it really isn't. In that case, the $2 million in savings is more to support a higher level of discretionary spending during retirement.

The big issue is that the average couple has just over $600,000, and at a 5% withdrawal rate, that is only $30,000 a year, which is getting too tight.

Meanwhile, Social Security's trust fund is expected to be partially depleted by 2033, which could result in a roughly 20%-25% cut to Social Security benefits if Congress doesn't act. The country will need to make important decisions about the future of Social Security, including how it is funded and how generous the benefits will be.

Accessing your home equity can help cover the average retirement account shortfall and offset any potential reduction in SSI, so we must discuss it as part of your retirement strategy.

Having access to additional funds ensures you have a better quality of life in retirement, can help others if needed, and won't outlive your savings. *Isn't this worth looking into?*

If it makes you feel any better, the issues we are having with retirement are not just an American issue. Worldwide, most industrial countries are dealing with this, and reverse mortgages are gaining in popularity across the globe.

Top Countries Utilizing Reverse Mortgages:

United States: The U.S. has the largest reverse mortgage market in the world, but one of the most underutilized by the population. The Home Equity Conversion Mortgage (HECM), insured by the Federal Housing Administration (FHA), accounts for most of them.

United Kingdom: The UK accounts for about three-quarters of the European reverse mortgage market, also known as *"equity release"* products. Almost 33% of all eligible senior homeowners in the UK have a reverse mortgage, making the UK the highest user of them percentage-wise.

Canada: The market has grown, with notable uptake of products like Home Equity Bank's CHIP reverse mortgage.

Australia: Despite a significant contraction after the 2008 financial crisis, the market has seen investment growth. The government has also encouraged the use of these products to help seniors *"age in place."*

South Korea: The market has experienced rapid adoption growth as part of government efforts to address the needs of an aging population.

Regional Trends and Other Markets:

Asia-Pacific: This region is experiencing the highest Compound Annual Growth Rate (CAGR) in reverse mortgage demand, driven by aging populations and rising property values, particularly in Japan, South Korea, and Australia.

Europe: While the UK dominates, other markets with notable activity include Spain and Ireland.

Emerging Markets: China (yes, Communist China!) is showing high interest in these products, while Mexico and Peru introduced them in 2016 and 2018, respectively.

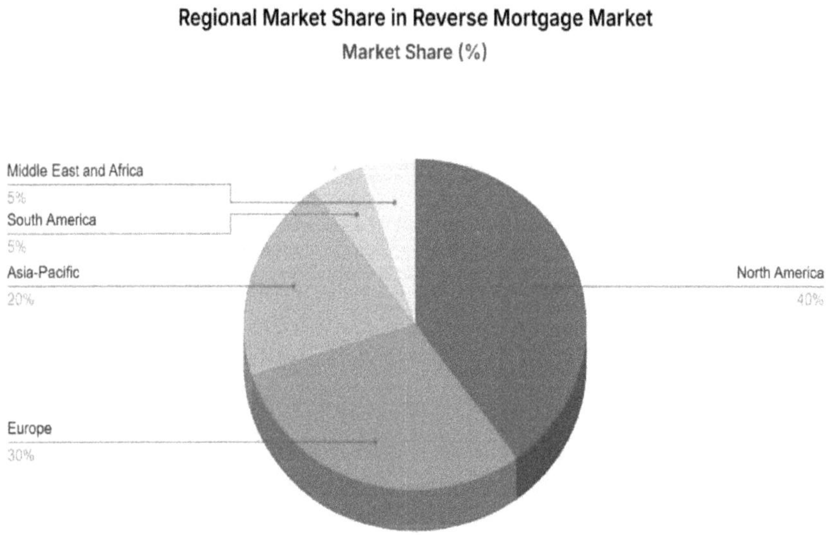

Key Drivers of Adoption:

The growth of these products is driven by:

- **Aging Populations:** A global increase in retirees with high home equity but low cash income.
- **Economic Pressures:** Inflation and the Need to Fund Long-Term Care.
- **Regulatory Support:** Improved, more secure, and regulated products are increasing consumer confidence.

Here is a great exercise for you. If you have not done anything like this, or it has been a while, fill in as much information below as possible to get a snapshot of your financial condition right now.

Then let's look at what it may be like in 20 years. To determine the costs over 20 years, we will use an annual inflation rate of 2.5%. With this rate, in 20 years, $1 will need to be about $1.60 to have the same purchasing power. This means multiplying each number you currently entered by 1.6 to get an estimate of the costs in 20 years.

Some costs will go away, which is good. Unfortunately, if you are a couple, one of you will pass away at some point. You may want to consider, in 20 years, what the reduced income would look like if one of you were to pass away.

This does not account for any health issues that may require additional healthcare costs or home services. If you want, calculate an additional $6,500 a month over 20 years to estimate those costs. Right now, they are averaging over $4K a month.

There is a scale for Financial Comfort on the sheet. When you look at your 20-year projected income/assets/expenses, how well do you feel you are prepared to live life comfortably? 1 being the most comfortable and 10 being you know you are not comfortable at all. If you are not in the 1-3 range on this scale, you should consider a reverse mortgage. If you are higher than 5 on the scale, you should definitely consider getting a reverse mortgage as soon as you can.

You can calculate the numbers out for 30 years, but your expenses go up more due to health issues. Use $9,000 per month to cover increased healthcare costs.

Income Per Month	Take Home Amount (after Tax)	
	Current	In 20 Years
1. SSI		
2. Pension		
3. 401k Distribution		
4. Annuity		
5. Job		
6. Business		
7. Rental Income		
8. Family Support		
9. Other		
Total Monthly Income		
Total Yearly Income		
	Current	In 20 Years
Monthly Expenditures		
1. Mortgage		
2. Taxes & Insurance		
3. Electricity & Gas		
4. Water		
5. Garbage		
6. Home Phone & Cell Phone		
7. Cable		
8. Internet		
9. Car Payment,Insurance,Register		
10. Gas		
11. Monthly Groceries		
12. Monthly Prescriptions		
13. Health Insurance		
14. Entertainment		
15. Travel		
16. Gifts for Family & Friends		
17. Credit Cards		
18. Pets (Food, Care, Vet)		
19. College Fund		
20. Monthly Subscriptions		
21. Other/Unexpected Expenses		
	Current	In 20 Years
Total Monthly Expenditures		
Number of Months Bank Reserves		

Date: ________

Prepared For:

____

____

Financial Comfort

1 being very comfortable

10 being very uncomfortable

1 2 3 4 5 6 7 8 9 10

CURRENT

Monthly +/-

In 20 Years+/-

3.

Why Use a Reverse Mortgage?

We will get into some fine details in a moment, but for now, I will discuss a broader overview of the different needs we all have in retirement.

We can define how our lives look by our current needs, desired lifestyle, and how we plan for the future we want to have.

What makes discussing these hard to quantify is that they look different for everyone. Some people want to live simple, quiet lives with days that are slow and peaceful, while others have needs that make them crave more to do in order to occupy themselves with many social activities, adventures, and new experiences.

Both lifestyle types are right because it is your retirement, and you live it the way you want to, not according to someone else's idea of retirement.

The problems come when you are not sure you can financially maintain the retirement you want. A reverse mortgage is a great tool to help you realize that lifestyle. Let's break this down some.

The first thing we need to look at is your current needs.

If we can't take care of the fundamentals, then there is a problem. Many people will struggle in retirement because they didn't save enough, and if they were honest with themselves, they would admit it. This is why using your home equity is so important for retirement planning. It is the largest asset you own that can bridge the gap from what you have to what you need.

If you have a mortgage and it is large, you may be better off using a reverse mortgage to pay it off. Let's look closer at this. For our example, let's say you have a $1,500-a-month mortgage payment. That is $18K a year. Let's also assume you have 5 years left on the mortgage. That is $90,000 you pay out of pocket, and $90,000 less, you can contribute towards your retirement, plus any gains you would have received. What did you do instead? You locked that $90,000 into your home, and unless you access it, you will never benefit from it.

If you have $400,000 in retirement savings and you take 4.5% out annually, that will be $18,000. The $18,000 a year in payments you locked into your home would have been the same as a $400,000 portfolio paying you 4.5% a year. You are currently paying the bank that money, but with a reverse mortgage, you would be paying yourself instead.

Ongoing home maintenance is another need that doesn't go away. Stay in a home long enough, and the roof, HVAC, appliances, painting, and all other home upkeep items will eventually need to be done all over again.

Same with transportation, supplemental healthcare plans, the rising costs of food, utilities, property taxes, insurance, and so on.

The next part we look into is your desired lifestyle.

Why did you retire? Sure, no one wants to work forever, and at some point, you just say I have had enough. But what are you doing next? You were so busy doing the day-to-day motions of living the life you were accustomed to, but did you really think long and hard about the kind of retirement you were about to enter for the rest of your life?

Were you financially prepared to live that lifestyle? If so, great! If you are not sure or you know you will fall short of that desired retirement, then using your home equity makes so much sense.

Socializing, traveling, time with family, and maybe even some peace of mind when emergencies arise can all be mitigated with the cash from a reverse mortgage. This access to additional money can afford you to live the quality of life that aligns with what you want.

Planning for your future.

If you are a couple, what happens when one of you passes away? Will the other be able to maintain the quality of life they want?

As you age, healthcare costs will take an increasingly larger percentage from your savings, and that will eventually become, by far, your largest expense. If you are not financially prepared for this, then your savings will get depleted rapidly.

If you plan to downsize soon, then is it better to pay for the new home all in cash or use a reverse mortgage to help pay for the new home, and you take the amount you save and put it back into your savings?

Stock market volatility creates stress for retirees. When the market is up, you feel fine, but get a couple of bad years, and you are drawing from your accounts when they are down, then you feel miserable. Using your home equity through a reverse mortgage can help offset the down years by letting you avoid taking cash out of your savings during those times. Instead, you can use the funds from the reverse mortgage and give your portfolio time to recover those losses.

There are many other examples I can use to explain why you would want to use a reverse mortgage to help you in retirement, but I think you can see the benefits by now. We'll go deeper into the strategies behind what we discussed and look at the pros and cons.

Why Reverse Mortgages Are Soaring in Popularity Again.

According to the National Reverse Mortgage Lenders Association, reverse mortgages jumped 6.23% in 2025. A report by Grand View Research projects the reverse mortgage market to reach $2.71 billion by 2030.

So why is the interest in reverse mortgages increasing?

More Seniors to Borrow-

The Census Bureau notes that seniors already outnumber children in nearly half of U.S. counties. A prior Census projection forecasts that they'll do so nationwide by 2034.

Home Equity and Cost of Living are Both Rising-

Home prices skyrocketed during and after the pandemic, shooting up 54.9% from early 2020 to early 2025, per the National Association of Home Builders. That supercharged many seniors' home equity.

Inflation has also sent the cost of everything else soaring as well, leaving many retirees house-rich but cash-poor.

Prices for everyday living, including food, utilities, gasoline, and health insurance, have increased substantially, and retirees reliant on fixed incomes are seeing their dollar buy less.

Loss of Income.

Not every retiree made an intentional decision to leave the workforce.

People look into reverse mortgages after losing a job, or the premature death of a spouse, and the loss of their Social Security benefits.

And in a labor market that discriminates against an older population, finding a new retirement job doesn't always happen quickly—if at all.

Purchase a second home or add an addition to your home.

With enough equity in your existing home, retirees can buy a second home without a down payment using an HECM for Purchase loan. That can help you spend part of the year closer to family or buy a vacation home.

You can even use reverse mortgages to build an accessory dwelling unit (ADU) for your existing home, if local regulations allow for it.

The homeowner can collect rent from the ADU while also avoiding a mortgage payment for a cash flow win-win.

A reverse mortgage can be more than a last-resort option. When used strategically, it may serve as a financial bridge that allows retirees to delay Social Security and potentially increase their lifetime income (cash flow).

For the right homeowner, this approach can improve cash flow flexibility, protect investments, and strengthen long-term retirement security.

Why Retirement Income Cash Flow Matters More Than Savings.

Retirement income (cash flow), not savings, pays your bills. What you spend matters more than what you save. If your spending outpaces your projections for how long your savings will last, then you have an issue. You either need to spend less, get access to more cash, or both.

Retirees focus more on a magic number for savings, but it is spending that will deplete their savings in retirement. Tapping into your home equity and using a reverse mortgage increases your savings and cash flow, so you have a much better chance of not outliving your savings. This is called Longevity Risk.

Longevity Risk is simply the chance of you living longer than your money. The longer you live, the more market volatility, emergencies, healthcare costs, and inflation eat away at your savings.

The faster you withdraw your savings, the greater the long-term risk you are exposed to.

Factors That Shape Withdrawal Rates.

Retirement spending is one of the great financial puzzles. After years of saving, the question shifts from "How much can I put away?" to "How much can I spend without running out?" When it comes to taking money out of a retirement portfolio, there is no single "right" answer.

For decades, the so-called 4% rule has been the rule of thumb. The "safe withdrawal rate," rooted in William Bengen's groundbreaking research, depends on a variety of moving parts. Understanding these variables not only explains why there is no single correct number but also shows why inflation risk rises above the rest.

The Drivers of Safe Withdrawal Rates

While the 4% rule is a useful starting point, Bengen's deeper work shows that sustainable withdrawals are conditional, not fixed. It helps to think of them as the dials on a control panel; move one, and the whole outcome changes. In his original analysis, withdrawals were inflation-adjusted over a 30-year horizon from a tax-advantaged account, rebalanced annually, with no explicit legacy target.

Through his research, Bengen identified eight elements that have an outsized impact on how much retirees can safely withdraw. Each one alters the math in different ways:

- **Withdrawal method**. Fixed dollar amounts, fixed percentages, or inflation-linked spending all produce very different outcomes.
- **Planning horizon**. Designing for longer-than-expected lifespans is critical. Adding 30-40 percent to a life expectancy estimate creates a safety buffer.
- **Account type**. Withdrawals from taxable accounts versus IRAs or other tax-deferred vehicles change the after-tax amount available.
- **Legacy goals**. Preserving wealth for heirs reduces what's available for ongoing spending.
- **Asset allocation**. The stock-to-bond mix is central to growth potential and volatility. A meaningful equity allocation is usually required to keep pace with inflation.
- **Rebalancing frequency**. Resetting allocations, typically once per year, helps portfolios stay aligned with their intended strategy.
- **Market approach**. Whether you stick with index returns or try to beat the market affects long-term sustainability.

- **Withdrawal timing**. Monthly withdrawals leave the portfolio slightly earlier than annual ones, trimming longevity by a measurable amount.

These drivers all matter, but one consistently overshadows the rest.

Why Inflation Overshadows the Rest

Among all the factors, inflation consistently emerges as the central risk. Bengen flags "high" inflation (5% or above) as especially damaging because it ratchets dollar withdrawals higher and keeps them there. Unlike a bear market, which eventually recovers, inflation locks in higher spending rates that rarely revert.

History makes the point clear. Retirees starting in the late 1960s faced high stock market valuations and inflation above 5%. Their portfolios were hit from both sides: muted returns and rising expenses. Over the following decade, their purchasing power fell by nearly three-quarters.

More recently, the early 2020s offered a reminder. After years of assuming inflation would stay tame, households suddenly faced annual increases above eight percent, with a peak above nine percent in mid-2022. Even though markets eventually rebounded, day-to-day living costs jumped permanently, forcing many retirees to withdraw more than planned.

Episodes like this underscore that inflation is not just background noise. It can redefine the entire retirement landscape.

The research makes clear that inflation deserves priority attention among retirement risks. While asset allocation, withdrawal rules, and account types all matter, none of them carries the same lasting impact as rising prices. A diversified portfolio with meaningful equity exposure helps keep pace with long-term costs over time, but flexibility is just as important. Retirees who adjust spending during inflationary spikes are better positioned to preserve their plans.

Why Essential vs. Discretionary Income Matters

Essential expenses support life and longevity. These are the costs you cannot afford to miss. Failing to cover them introduces stress that compounds quickly and can permanently undermine a retirement plan. Discretionary expenses support Lifestyle. They enhance retirement while allowing flexibility. Spending can be adjusted without threatening long-term financial security. This difference is less about labeling expenses and more about deciding which risks you are willing to accept.

This classification matters because it determines how assets are invested and protected. Reliable income sources that are not tied to market performance are best suited to essential expenses. These costs need to be paid regardless of market conditions. Market-dependent assets are better suited for discretionary goals. When markets perform well, lifestyle spending can increase. When markets struggle, adjustments can be made without jeopardizing the foundation of the plan.

This is often where retirees start realizing their plan looks good on paper but seems fragile in practice. Without this clarity, retirees may feel forced to take more risk than they are comfortable with, or they may underestimate how stressful volatility is on their savings, and the amount they can safely withdraw is diminished.

Let's take a look at some common risks in retirement.

As I mentioned earlier, Longevity Risk:

The good news: Advances in medicine and healthier lifestyles mean that people are living longer than ever.

The not"as-good" news: Increased longevity means increased longevity risk. The reality is you could spend as much or more time in retirement than you spent at work. To reduce the risk of outliving your savings, you may need to grow it to last for 30+ years of retirement income—especially if you end up retiring earlier than you had planned.

Inflation Risk:

Many of us underestimate the eroding effect inflation can have on our savings over time. Yet retirees may struggle to maintain their desired lifestyle as living expenses such as food, housing, and healthcare continue to increase over time, eroding their savings. Over a 20- to 30-year retirement, that erosion, sometimes called purchasing power risk, can dramatically change your lifestyle.

Volatility Risk:

Volatility risk refers to the potential impact of unpredictable market fluctuations on your retirement portfolio. Unlike inflation or longevity risk, which tend to follow longer-term trends, volatility can be sudden, emotional, and often amplified by media headlines.

Emotion Risk:

Emotion risk is the impact of fear, regret, or overconfidence on decision-making. Unlike volatility or inflation, it doesn't show up on a financial statement, but it can quietly undermine even the best retirement plan.

Retirement is an emotional, not just financial, experience: Identity loss, changing routines, and health concerns influence how you make decisions.

4.

How the Reverse Mortgage Works.

There are different kinds of reverse mortgages in the US. Some private lenders offer proprietary reverse mortgages, and they each have their own terms and conditions on how they work and who qualifies for them. Although they have their place in the market, I will concentrate most of the time on the FHA-insured Home Equity Conversion Mortgage (HECM) administered by the Department of Housing & Urban Development.

I will say that in some cases, proprietary reverse mortgages may be a better option. Home values above $1.3 million, borrowers under 62, and non-HUD-approved condominiums are good examples of situations in which these products may be more suitable for borrowers.

Since they all have different underwriting guidelines and qualifications associated with them, it is easier to discuss the HECM. It is the most popular reverse mortgage product in the U.S., and in most cases, it is the most suitable for the majority of seniors.

At least one borrower must be 62 years old, but if there is a younger spouse, they can be included as a non-borrowing spouse (NBS). The amount of cash available will always be based on the age of the youngest borrower or the NBS, but only the borrower has access to any additional funds available. The point of the legal designation of an NBS is that if something were to happen to the borrower, say they passed away, the NBS can remain in the home for the rest of their life or until they decide to vacate the home, so they are protected from being evicted to pay off the loan.

The borrower does not have any monthly payments they are obligated to pay the lender. The loan will get paid back, along with any accumulated interest and loan fees, by the estate after either all borrowers pass away or until the last borrower vacates the home.

There are still obligations that need to be met. As with any responsible home ownership, property taxes must be paid, homeowner's insurance must be in force as the home is the collateral for the loan, maintenance and property upkeep must be kept up, and if you belong to an HOA, those fees need to be paid, and any violations need to be cured.

Borrowers can own more than one property (there is no limit to how many properties they can own), but the property on which they get the HECM must be their primary home.

The credit score is not calculated in qualifying for the loan, but the credit history is. If the borrower has a recent bankruptcy, foreclosure, or derogatory credit that cannot be explained adequately, then that may impact their ability to qualify for the loan and/or how much they can receive.

We do not need to demonstrate having enough money to make monthly payments since there are none. Still, we do need to show that the borrower has sufficient funds monthly so that they can take care of themselves, so there is a minimum monthly residual income needed after income and debt are calculated. The amount varies by region and the number of people living in the home. Most married borrowers will qualify for the loan on Social Security income alone.

If there is a mortgage, judgement or any other liens on the property, the HECM must pay them off in full before the borrower has any additional funds available to them. Almost all reverse mortgages require this, but there are a few proprietary reverse mortgages that will allow you to keep your mortgage and give you some more cash as a second lien on the property.

HUD counseling is mandatory for all reverse mortgages. Counseling is a consumer protection feature and must be provided by an approved, certified HUD counselor, either over the phone or in person. Anyone on the title and all borrowers and NBS must get the counseling. The purpose of the counseling is to ensure that the information the borrower receives from the loan officer is truthful and accurate, and since the counselor does not get paid for you to do the loan, they are an objective source to answer all your questions.

They are also evaluating the borrower's capacity to understand the loan and ensure they are suitable for it.

There are multiple ways to take the funds that are available to the borrower. The interest rate that accrues on the loan can either be fixed or adjustable. Most HECMs are adjustable, as they offer more cash and flexibility in how you can take the money. I will discuss the adjustable options first.

1. ***A line of credit (LOC):*** This is an account that holds the funds until the borrower requests them. There is no obligation for the borrower to take any of the funds at any time, and as long as they meet all the terms and conditions of the loan, the LOC will remain available until the last borrower passes away or vacates the home. My favorite feature of the HECM line of credit is that there is a tax-free growth rate associated with it. Meaning that all available funds in the LOC grow annually, so the amount increases every year. This is guaranteed and is not correlated to the value of the home or market performance. HUD put this in place as an incentive for borrowers to save as much as possible, knowing that more funds would be available later. This is very impactful for retirement planning, and I will get into it in more detail later on.

2. ***Tenure:*** This option guarantees the borrower an equal monthly payment amount for life, no matter how long they live, even if the loan balance exceeds the home value. The tenure payment functions very much like a lifetime annuity payment. This is a good option if you want or need a steady, predictable income for life. The good thing is you can change the amount needed at any time if you need to, but be aware that increasing the monthly amount later on means it may not last for life.
3. ***Term:*** This option offers set monthly payments for a specific, pre-determined period of time. Unlike tenure payments, the amount will not last for life. The more you take monthly, the less time it will last. This is a good option if you have a specific timeline you need the money for. Maybe you will have an annuity or another pool of money available to you in 5 or 10 years, and you only need the cash from the HECM until that other source becomes available. Maybe you are paying off a student loan, an automobile loan, or a mortgage on a second home, and you only need the HECM payments until the other payment ends. Some people delay taking Social Security and continue receiving monthly HECM payments until SSI kicks in later. We will go into this more later on.
4. ***Full cash out:*** This is geared towards the fixed rate option. With a fixed rate, your only option is to take all available cash at closing, or you lose the amount you do not take. You also

get less money unless you have a large mortgage balance to pay off. If you have no mortgage, then you only get 60% of the available cash that an adjustable-rate option offers. There are no term, tenure, or LOC options available with the fixed rate.

To qualify for the HECM loan, the property also must meet certain criteria.

1. The property must be the borrower's primary residence.
2. It must be a 1-4 unit residential property, a townhome, an approved HUD condominium, or a qualified manufactured home. No commercial properties, vacation homes, investment properties, or farms are allowed.
3. The total mortgage/lien balance on the home must be low enough for the HECM to pay it off in full. There can be no remaining balances against the home at the time of closing of the HECM. You can possibly have a 2nd lien on the home after the HECM is in place, but that is up to each individual lender and has nothing to do with the original HECM lender.
4. The property must meet all HUD/FHA underwriting guidelines, and an appraisal must be completed for the loan to determine the valuation and suitability of the property.

Fees related to the loan.

There are three buckets of fees for the HECM. Almost all of them can be rolled into the loan.

1. ***Origination fee:*** This is from the lender, and it is what the lender charges to do the loan. The max fee that can be charged as of 2026 is $6,000.
2. ***Third-party fees***: These are fees that are charged by third parties and are required to get the loan approved. They can include, but are not limited to: title fees, attorney fees, appraisal fees, state, county & city taxes, trust reviews, a counseling fee, or any other costs required to complete the loan.
3. ***Initial Mortgage Insurance Premium*** (IMIP). This is the one that most people don't really understand very well, and it is the largest fee that gets rolled into the loan. It is calculated at 2% of the property's appraised value. It is not homeowner's or title insurance. This is a one-time fee the FHA charges to insure the loan. This fee is only for the FHA HECM; proprietary reverse mortgages are not insured by the FHA, so they do not charge this fee. The IMIP is very important as the insurance has several benefits.

The government insures the loan and guarantees the lender they will get paid in full. The guarantee is the reason the lender does not require the borrower to make any monthly payments. It also guarantees that the money to the borrower will always be available. If the lender goes out of business at any time, the FHA will step in and reassign the full amount available to you to another lender.

a. Non-recourse protection. It guarantees that if the loan balance exceeds the home's value when the loan becomes due, the insurance covers the difference, since only the home can be used to repay the loan. This prevents lenders from seeking repayment from the borrower's other assets in their estate or their heirs' personal funds if the home value is less than the loan balance. This is very important. No one will ever go into debt paying off the loan. Even if the estate has millions in other assets, they cannot be used to pay back any of the loan balance, so those other assets are protected.

Non-Borrowing Spouse (NBS).

There are times when the loan will only be made out to one spouse, such as when only one of you is 62 or older, they may not live at home and are in a nursing home, there financial situation is bad enough that you would not qualify for the loan so it is only made out to one of you, and some other cases.

There are two types of NBS: Eligible and Non-Eligible.

Eligible NBS simply means that if the borrower were to pass away or vacate the home (such as a divorce or move into a nursing home), the NBS can remain in the home for the rest of their lives and not have to pay any of the money owed back. The loan gets paid back when they pass away or vacate the home. The only issue with the NBS is that the loan is only made out to the borrower, so the NBS cannot access any future funds. The NBS would need to refinance the loan in its name to access additional funds.

A non-NBS is someone who is not protected from the loan being called after the borrower passes or vacates the home. Some examples of this include the borrower getting married after taking out the reverse mortgage (the new spouse was never on the loan documents) or, for medical reasons, the spouse not living at the home as their primary residence.

This means they will need to either refinance the loan in their name, through a reverse mortgage or a traditional home loan, or sell the home to repay the money owed to the lender.

When the loan gets paid back.

Once all the borrowers or eligible NBS pass away or leave the home, the clock is ticking, and the loan will eventually need to be paid back. Per federal guidelines, the initial amount of time the estate has to pay back the loan is 180 days, but two 90-day extensions are allowed and must be approved by the servicing company. Most often, the servicer will work with the estate if more time is needed.

The borrowers receive monthly statements throughout the life of the loan, showing the updated balance, so the estate has a record of the amount due and the contact information of the servicing company to settle the loan.

The heirs of the estate can either keep the home or sell it; that decision is up to the heirs.

If they want to keep it, they must pay the loan back. They can do this through traditional financing, a reverse mortgage (if they and the property qualify), or from their own funds.

If they want to sell the home, then they pay what is owed at closing. If the loan is more than what the home is worth, the estate only needs to pay back 95% of the appraised value of the home.

5.

Integrating Your Home Equity with Other Retirement Sources.

One of the great things about the HECM is its versatility and how you can incorporate it into your retirement to maximize other sources of retirement income. You can receive more money over time and preserve the cash you have saved for a longer duration in retirement.

Let's look at how you can use it to better maximize your social security income.

Claiming Social Security early can make sense in certain situations, such as a single individual who is in poor health, someone with limited savings, or other planning circumstances, such as having young or disabled children. But for many people, claiming early may do more harm than good.

The decision is personal, and everyone's reason for taking SSI varies. Still, considering the trade-offs, it is often wiser long-term to wait until Full Retirement Age (FRA) if possible. Here's why.

Despite some headlines, the Social Security Fund's facing partial insolvency does not mean Social Security would stop paying benefits.

If Social Security reserves were depleted, benefits would still be paid from ongoing payroll taxes and other income, though they could be reduced. The current projections have it being reduced by around 20%-25% by 2033. The program has faced funding challenges before, and Congress has stepped in to address them to avoid benefit cuts.

Claiming early permanently reduces your base benefit; claiming before any future reductions would occur due to insolvency does not grandfather the claimant from future exposure. The reduced benefit would be reduced once again, only adding to the strain on other sources of retirement savings to make up the difference.

Claiming Social Security before your Full Retirement Age permanently reduces your monthly benefit. Waiting until Full Retirement Age (FRA) allows you to receive 100% of your earned benefit, and delaying beyond FRA increases it further through delayed retirement credits.

A smaller benefit also means smaller COLAs forever.

Cost-of-living adjustments are applied as a percentage of your benefit, so a higher monthly benefit matters. Claiming early not only reduces your monthly check but also shrinks the dollar impact of every future COLA for the rest of your life.

Your claiming age also matters to your spouse.

For married couples, especially when one spouse is the higher earner, claiming decisions affect more than one lifetime. A surviving spouse may receive up to 100% of the benefit the deceased worker was receiving or entitled to receive, including delayed retirement credits. That makes the higher earner's claiming age a critical factor in long-term survivor income. An early claim by the higher-earning spouse translates to a smaller survivor benefit.

Using the money from a reverse mortgage line of credit can help you wait until you reach FRA, so you get to maximize your full SSI. Instead of drawing the additional money from your savings from when you retire to the FRA, you use the equity from your home with the HECM. You can now allow the savings in your retirement accounts to continue to grow each year, and that will hopefully result in more cash in your savings.

For example, let's say you retire at age 62, but the FRA is 67. There is a five-year gap until you reach the FRA. Let's say that the monthly SS payment at FRA will be $3,000. What you do is wait to take SSI until you are 67 and, in the meantime, you take out $3,000 a month or $36,000 annually from the reverse mortgage until you turn 67. Then, at 67, you stop taking the monthly reverse mortgage payment and start taking the $3,000 monthly SSI benefit.

Not only are you receiving more each month for the rest of your life, but you have saved $180,000 from your savings and all the interest it would have accumulated during those five years.

Also, if any of the money from your retirement accounts were taxable, you save yourself from having to spend more money to pay taxes on those withdrawals and possibly land you in a higher tax bracket. You took the extra $36,000, which is declared income, so getting bumped up into a higher tax bracket means you pay more taxes not only on the $36,000 you withdrew but on all the money you earned for that year.

The reverse mortgage money is not taxable and is not considered earned income, so it will not bump you up into a higher tax bracket.

More cash in savings, a higher monthly SS payment, and a higher COLA all add up to more money now and in the future, and a higher death benefit for the surviving spouse.

Here is another example of an actual borrower I helped just before writing this book.

A couple in New York with an $800,000 home value, both age 62, opened a Reverse Mortgage line of credit (LOC) with a starting amount of $234,000. At today's rates, the growth annually on that LOC is currently about 6.63%, and the growth is tax-free, and the distributions are also tax-free.

Using the Reverse Mortgage LOC from age 65 to age 70, when they want to start taking SSI, will bridge that gap without them taking that money from their savings. They saved $240,000 from their retirement savings during that time, and if that money were to grow at 7% annually, then it would increase to $336,612 during that time period. That money also continues to grow throughout their retirement years.

Annual Growth Table

Year	Value
0 (Start)	**$240,000.00**
Year 1	$256,800.00
Year 2	$274,776.00
Year 3	$294,010.32
Year 4	$314,591.04
Year 5	**$336,612.42**

Growth Details- 7% annually.

- **Total Growth**: $96,612.42.
- **Percentage Increase**: Approximately 40.26% over the 5-year period.

	Year	Interest Rate	Other Disbursement	Total Disbursement	LOC
0	2026	6.63	0	0	234,419
1	2027	6.63	0	0	251,678
2	2028	6.63	0	0	270,207
3	2029	6.63	48,000	48,000	242,101
4	2030	6.63	48,000	96,000	211,925
5	2031	6.63	48,000	144,000	179,528
6	2032	6.63	48,000	192,000	144,745
7	2033	6.63	48,000	240,000	107,402

You can see it reduced the LOC amount available to around $107,000, but that is temporary.

What happens to your income when one of you passes away?

When both spouses are alive, it is much easier to manage month-to-month expenses. When one spouse passes, then expenses can get out of hand quickly if you have limited savings or you are trying to preserve the savings you have. Ongoing fixed expenses increase over time, and Social Security statistics show that when a household loses one Social Security recipient, the overall reduction is between 30%-50%. If you draw from your current savings, then you are depleting your retirement accounts at an accelerated rate, which is bad for longevity.

Using our example earlier with the couple maximizing their Social Security benefits at 70 years old, let's move forward in time 15 years later and look at how the LOC can help our borrowers again. We will continue with the same borrowers, but at 85 years old, one of them passes away, and the surviving spouse wants to make up for the lost monthly income.

In the table below, we see that the LOC over those 15 years is estimated to have grown to $311,739. We will say that the surviving spouse wants to take out $4,000 a month to start with, and after five years, due to inflation, they increase that to $5,000 a month.

If you look at the table below, you can see that they can maintain that withdrawal rate for 8 years total, or until age 93. This is strictly using the Reverse Mortgage LOC and does not take into account income from SSI, any insurance death benefits, and withdrawals from their retirement assets.

	Year	Interest Rate	Other Disbursement	Total Disbursement	LOC
0	2026	6.63	0	0	234,419
1	2027	6.63	0	0	251,678
2	2028	6.63	0	0	270,207
3	2029	6.63	48,000	48,000	242,101
4	2030	6.63	48,000	96,000	211,925
5	2031	6.63	48,000	144,000	179,528
6	2032	6.63	48,000	192,000	144,745
7	2033	6.63	48,000	240,000	107,402
8	2034	6.63	0	240,000	115,309
9	2035	6.63	0	240,000	123,798
10	2036	6.63	0	240,000	132,913
11	2037	6.63	0	240,000	142,698
12	2038	6.63	0	240,000	153,204
13	2039	6.63	0	240,000	164,484
14	2040	6.63	0	240,000	176,594
15	2041	6.63	0	240,000	189,595
16	2042	6.63	0	240,000	203,554
17	2043	6.63	0	240,000	218,540
18	2044	6.63	0	240,000	234,630
19	2045	6.63	0	240,000	251,904
20	2046	6.63	0	240,000	270,450
21	2047	6.63	0	240,000	290,361
22	2048	6.63	0	240,000	311,739
23	2049	6.63	48,000	288,000	286,690
24	2050	6.63	48,000	336,000	259,797
25	2051	6.63	48,000	384,000	230,924
26	2052	6.63	48,000	432,000	199,926
27	2053	6.63	48,000	480,000	166,645
28	2054	6.63	60,000	540,000	118,914
29	2055	6.63	60,000	600,000	67,669
30	2056	6.63	60,000	660,000	12,651
31	2057	6.63	0	660,000	13,582
	Total:		660,000.00		

The combination of the borrowers talking money out of the LOC due to the delayed SSI and supplementing the loss of income during a total of 30 years is a total of $660,000.

Meanwhile, the available funds in their retirement accounts are allowed to grow and increase the likelihood that their money will last them throughout their entire lives. You can see how the Reverse Mortgage LOC benefits the borrowers and helps to preserve their retirement assets.

Not only is this good for retirement longevity, but it can also help with estate planning.

They may be able to increase insurance coverage for riders to handle long-term care costs or increased death benefits. This ensures that the heirs stand to inherit what is left in their retirement accounts and what the death benefit is on the insurance policy.

This is a good idea because the money borrowed from the reverse mortgage will need to be paid back when the borrowers pass. Only the home can be used to pay back the loan, so all other assets in the estate are protected. This is a benefit to the heirs because if the home value is less than the loan amount (underwater), the estate will not need to come up with additional funds to make up the difference. The FHA insurance will cover any loan shortfall.

The borrowers get more cash to live off of, their retirement assets have more opportunity to grow, and the heirs can still get a substantial inheritance.

Everyone wins!

Investment accounts are not designed for individuals to make life decisions in emotionally charged moments. The surviving spouse must deal with market volatility and take withdrawals during a portfolio loss. They must manage the accounts alone, making decisions that can be stressful and possibly leading to conflicting advice from family, friends, and financial professionals.

Guaranteed income from a reverse mortgage can help relieve the surviving spouse of many of these issues. Withdrawing money from the reverse mortgage lessens any negative impact that living on one reduced total SS income may have on them and still allows them to preserve their retirement funds because they do not need to take as much out in a down market. All of the reverse mortgage income is tax-free and does not affect any of your federal benefits!

Traveling in Retirement

Many people want to travel early on in retirement, while they still are healthy enough to do that, but are concerned about taking too much out of their savings early. They are rightfully concerned that doing this will deplete their retirement funds faster than they planned.

Again, you earned the right to pursue the retirement you want, and isn't one of the main reasons people retire to begin with to pursue their interests in what makes them happy? After working and/or raising a family for decades, this is not an unreasonable expectation.

Traveling isn't always about visiting exotic places and crossing off an experience from your bucket list. Sometimes it is as simple as wanting to spend more time with family or friends who may be scattered across the country. Attending grandchildren's events, being there for someone else who may be struggling and could use a friend during a difficult time.

My wife and I love to visit the national parks. We live in a beautiful country with so much biological and geographic diversity. It is not terribly expensive to travel within the U.S., but it still costs money. Maybe you just want to be in the company of the one you shared your life with, in a different setting, just relaxing on a beach or mountain cabin, and enjoy life.

The concern of spending too much too soon is a legitimate one, but it shouldn't stop you from living a good quality of life. How does a reverse mortgage help in this situation?

It all starts with a budget. If you know roughly how much you plan to spend traveling and for how many years, then it is easier to create a plan that will facilitate this. Let's use an example of $20,000 a year for your travel budget, and this will go on for at least 15 years. That is $300,000 total.

Instead of taking that out of your retirement funds, why not use your home equity? Use the $20K from your reverse mortgage line of credit to pay for your trips, so you preserve the cash in your retirement accounts. That $300K, plus any appreciation you would have earned over 15 years, will most likely be worth a lot more than the initial $300K, probably double that, depending on how much your assets grow during that time.

The same tax issues come into play as the SS example we discussed earlier. Paying taxes on withdrawn funds and possibly bumping you into a higher tax bracket on all your income.

Paying Taxes

I mentioned that withdrawals from some retirement accounts may require you to pay taxes on the money. Also, converting funds from a traditional IRA to a Roth IRA also has tax implications.

Rather than using your savings to pay those taxes, you can use the money from the reverse mortgage. This allows you to keep more cash in your savings account to grow over time.

If you have a business where a large tax bill is due, or you run into a situation where the cash flow is temporarily reduced, you can use the reverse mortgage funds to meet expenses and get you through that difficult period.

You can pay your property taxes and homeowner's insurance with the reverse mortgage funds, and if you own multiple properties, you can do this on all of them. This is very appealing in states with high property taxes.

Healthcare

Paying for out-of-pocket healthcare expenses is the second biggest reason people get a reverse mortgage. With the average couple expected to spend around $325K out of pocket for healthcare costs in retirement, this is a big pill to swallow for most retirees.

Understanding Your Healthcare Costs

Before you can manage healthcare costs, you need to understand what you're actually paying. A typical retiree's healthcare expenses fall into several categories.

2026 Medicare Cost Breakdown

Part B Premium $202.90/month ($2,435/year)

Part D Premium (average)$55/month ($660/year)

Medigap Plan G (average) $150/month ($1,800/year)

Medicare Savings Programs

Many retirees don't realize they may qualify for programs that help pay Medicare costs. These programs have higher income limits than you might expect. You can research this more at Medicare.gov.

Program What It Pays Income Limit (2026)

QMB Part A & B premiums, deductibles, and copays $1,275/month

SLMB Part B premium only $1,527/month

QI Part B premium only $1,715/month

Extra Help Part D premiums and drug costs $1,903/month

Paying to Age-in-Place

Three-quarters of older Americans said they want to age in place, according to AARP. Yet that comes with its own costs, including home modifications, caregivers, and rising healthcare bills. It also puts a strain on your family if they must help with any care you need.

A study from Finance of America finds that one-third of Americans aged 40-60 report feeling significant emotional, physical, and financial strain as they try to balance caring for both aging parents and children.

Within this group, men feel more financial pressure, and women are more inclined to bear emotional and physical caregiving burdens.

More than three-quarters of self-identified sandwich caregivers report being emotionally, physically, and financially exhausted.

29 percent expect multigenerational living (parents moving in), complicating space, budgets, and routines.

26 percent of respondents' parents hadn't planned on living this long, underscoring planning gaps.

21 percent have delayed life events (home ownership, marriage), rising to 45 percent among those who feel 'sandwiched.'

Open conversations about family finances make a measurable difference: 60 percent are less overwhelmed, 63 percent worry less, and 84 percent focus on what matters. A reverse mortgage needs to be part of that conversation and getting educated on how it can be used to help not only the borrower, but family caregivers as well.

Keep in mind that there is no guarantee the heirs will inherit the house.

The home may need to be sold to pay for assisted living or memory care if the care needed exceeds the capacity of a family caregiver.

MERP - Medicaid Estate Recovery Program: If Medicaid is used for long-term care (depending on the state), Medicaid has the right to lien the entire estate to be reimbursed for LTC costs.

Start planning for these events and have a reverse mortgage as part of that conversation.

Here are some potential uses for a reverse mortgage related to healthcare:

Replace lost income for family caregivers. It may come down to having a family member helping an aging parent or sibling when they are in declining health. This may put financial strain on the caregiver if they have to work less to help take care of you.

Respite care for family members. Sometimes the primary caregiver cannot be there, and temporary home care services may be needed.

Remodel the home to make it more disability and aging-in-place-friendly, making in-home care easier. Installing more accommodating beds, baths, and mobility aids for safety can get expensive.

Stop the bleeding of out-of-pocket expenses of family caregivers. Even if they are not missing income from work by taking care of you, they may still be paying for things out of their own income, and they should not be put in any financial difficulty by taking care of you.

Set up the reverse mortgage now so that the remaining spouse can live comfortably once assets are spent down and household income is lost.

Use reverse mortgage proceeds to pay for services such as grocery delivery, yard maintenance, housekeeping, a cook/meal prep, meal delivery, and transportation, relieving pressure on family members.

Estate planning—trust or will. I will get into this more later on.

Medicaid estate recovery planning. Better to discuss with an estate attorney.

Pay for adult day care.

If possible, use proceeds to increase insurance coverage for survivor benefits or for estate inheritance.

Use proceeds to cover medical supplies that Medicaid/Medicare won't cover.

Using a reverse mortgage with Medicaid requires careful planning because Medicaid is sensitive to your income. Let's talk about how to coordinate cash from a reverse mortgage with Medicaid-funded care—without losing Medicaid eligibility. Using an attorney or financial advisor early in the conversation is recommended.

Here's the key Medicaid planning insight:

The funds you receive from a reverse mortgage are not automatically treated as income by Medicaid. As long as those funds don't sit in a bank account and pile up, they generally don't count against the strict asset limits that determine Medicaid eligibility.

That means—with the right approach—you can use reverse mortgage proceeds to help cover home-based care, caregiving support, or other allowable expenses without disqualifying yourself from Medicaid coverage.

How this works in practice:

Don't let the money accumulate as cash on hand. Medicaid rules in most states require that loan proceeds be spent in the month they're received—otherwise, unspent funds may be counted as a countable asset and could put you over Medicaid's very low asset threshold.

Choose wisely how you receive the funds. Many advisors recommend taking reverse mortgage proceeds as monthly payments or a line of credit you draw on as needed. That way, you're more likely to spend the funds on care or living expenses before they become a problem at month's end.

Coordinate timing with the Medicaid application. If you're planning to apply for Medicaid, your attorney or financial planner can help time the reverse mortgage distribution so that proceeds don't jeopardize eligibility—and help you track expenses so funds are used in a Medicaid-friendly way.

Bottom line? A reverse mortgage doesn't have to be a threat to Medicaid benefits—it can be a bridge to keep you in your home and help pay for care. But it must be structured and managed strategically to avoid creating countable assets that push you out of eligibility.

Better tax, estate, and financial planning can happen when another source of income tax-free funds can be brought into the picture and planned around.

Estate Planning

Life Insurance and Reverse Mortgage Strategy.

Life insurance should be an essential part of every individual's financial plan. In your 30s-50s, it is particularly important if you have others depending on you, such as your spouse and children. For example, if you are the primary breadwinner in your house, you should have enough insurance to (at the very least) replace your income until your youngest child turns 18.

These days, life insurance is being used in countless ways to not only insure against a worst-case scenario, but also for tax planning, estate planning, and even for retirement. One very creative strategy is to combine a life insurance policy with a reverse mortgage.

To maximize this strategy, borrowers should have their homes paid off or have a remaining balance low enough to be satisfied with the proceeds from the reverse mortgage closing.

Which Type of Life Insurance works Best with a Reverse Mortgage?

There are two general forms of life insurance, term and permanent life. While term life insurance has significantly lower rates and works well for individuals who need a lot of insurance during their working years, it is generally not the best option to combine with a reverse mortgage. To ensure coverage will remain in effect for the life of the individual policyholder, it is best to have permanent life insurance.

The truth is that the reason term life insurance is so inexpensive is that insurance companies only pay out about 3% of all the policies. This is because the individuals almost always outlive the term. This makes them very lucrative for insurance companies but really bad for estate planning when the policy needs to be in effect for the entire life of all the insured, up until they pass away.

A Reverse Mortgage, paired with some form of insurance, will not only serve the borrower's needs but also provide a larger inheritance for their heirs. To ensure the policy is in force for the life of the insured, it is usually better to have some type of Permanent life insurance, so the borrower does not outlive the policy term. Using reverse mortgages and life insurance together can create liquidity, preserve other assets, and help protect heirs.

Term Life Insurance:

Term life insurance provides coverage for a specific period, typically 10, 20, or 30 years. It's the simplest form of life insurance: you pay premiums, and if you pass away during the term, your beneficiaries receive the death benefit. There's no cash value or investment component.

Most term policies require a medical exam during underwriting, which helps determine your premium based on health, age, and other factors. For those who can't afford permanent coverage or only need temporary protection, term is an efficient, affordable solution.

Term insurance is often the right choice for temporary protection needs.

Permanent Life Insurance:

Permanent life insurance provides lifelong coverage as long as premiums are paid. Unlike term, permanent policies include a cash value component—a savings feature that grows over time. Permanent insurance may be better for long-term goals and lifelong needs. When structured properly, it serves multiple purposes. There are several types of permanent insurance, each with different characteristics:

Whole Life Insurance:

Fixed premiums, guaranteed cash value growth, and potential dividends. This is the most predictable permanent option.

Universal Life Insurance:

Flexible premiums and adjustable death benefit. Cash value earns interest based on current rates.

Indexed Universal Life:

Cash value growth linked to market index performance with downside protection (0% floor).

Variable Universal Life:

Cash value invested in sub-accounts (like mutual funds). Higher growth potential but also exposed to more market risk—cash value can decrease, so it is risky to own in retirement and for estate planning.

How Cash Value Works:

Whole life; Guaranteed interest rate on cash value

Universal life; Based on current interest rate assumptions

Indexed universal life; Linked to an index like the S&P 500, with a floor protecting against losses

Variable universal life; Depends on the performance of the underlying investment sub-accounts.

Here is an example of a scenario wherein this strategy might work. A retired couple in their early 70s and in good health wants to tap into some extra money to help supplement their Social Security and pension during retirement. They own a house free and clear with a value of $600,000, and they qualify for a reverse mortgage line of credit of $250,000. To help cover the balance of the loan, they could take out a $250,000 guaranteed joint survivor universal life policy that would remain in effect as long as the monthly premiums are paid.

They can either pay for the monthly premiums with their retirement funds or the reverse mortgage line of credit. There are many factors that determine which funds are better to use, such as the performance of their retirement portfolio, the amount remaining in that portfolio, and what else they need the money for from the reverse mortgage line of credit.

Life insurance combined with a reverse mortgage is not for everyone, but it is a very innovative strategy for those in the right circumstances who want to safely cash in on the equity in their home and leave something more for their heirs. The equity the heirs lose from the reverse mortgage balance can be offset in part or in full by the insurance benefit. The insurance benefit is tax-free!

Notice I am only discussing life insurance and not annuities. There is a reason for this. Early in the book, I mentioned how some lenders got into regulatory trouble combining reverse mortgages with annuity sales.

The impetus for the regulations that separate annuities and reverse mortgages arose in the early days of the HECM reverse mortgage program when one or more HECM lenders combined with one or more annuity providers to offer loan/annuity combos to gullible seniors at extortionate terms. In response, HUD instructed counselors that potential borrowers must consult with them before submitting a loan application, and warned borrowers to beware of annuities. HUD also prohibited HECM lenders from having relationships with other financial institutions.

Federal law prohibits lenders from forcing borrowers to purchase annuities or life insurance as a condition for a reverse mortgage.

On the annuity side, because some early combination deals led to lawsuits against insurers by disgruntled heirs of HECM borrowers, the industry adopted the rule that annuities could not be financed with reverse mortgage proceeds. This doesn't prevent you from buying an annuity with your own funds, but you can't get a reverse mortgage with the intention of purchasing an annuity with the funds from the reverse mortgage. I am not discouraging anyone from purchasing an annuity with existing funds in their savings if it makes sense. There are benefits to utilizing a reverse mortgage and an annuity combination. Look at this example.

Consider the case of a 62-year-old male who owns a debt-free house worth $500,000 but has little in financial assets, making him house-rich but cash-poor.

His only stand-alone option is a HECM tenure payment, which provides a fixed monthly payment.

If, instead of taking the tenure payment, the borrower combines a HECM line of credit with an existing annuity on which payment is deferred 10 years, his monthly payment in this example will be $500. During the first 10 years, the payments would be drawn from the reverse mortgage credit line, afterward, they would then come from the annuity when the deferment period ends. The man gets payments from both sources after 10 years. Monthly payments on the annuity would continue until the borrower died. In contrast, the reverse mortgage monthly tenure payment continues and only terminates when the borrower dies or vacates the house, selling the home or moving into a nursing home, for example.

The same prohibited rules apply to purchasing single-premium life insurance products with reverse mortgage proceeds. Getting a reverse mortgage to fund a single premium life insurance product is not allowed, the same rule that applies to annuities.

Single premium life insurance (SPLI) is a permanent policy funded by one large lump-sum payment, providing immediate lifelong coverage without future premium payments.

This does not mean you can't buy life insurance; it states you should not purchase it in a lump sum. You can purchase life insurance that has monthly premiums because you can cancel it at any time.

The Role of Investments in Retirement

Investments provide flexibility and growth potential. When markets perform well, retirees can enjoy a higher standard of living, preserve liquidity for emergencies, and even grow their assets for legacy goals. Investments also allow for adjustments along the way, which can be helpful as life circumstances change.

The challenge is that relying entirely on investments comes with trade-offs. Sequence-of-returns risk is the risk that poor investment results early in retirement could permanently reduce sustainable income, even if markets recover later. Longevity risk, which is the possibility of living far longer than expected, requires retirees to spend cautiously, which often leads to underspending and the unintended consequence of leaving behind a larger-than-expected legacy.

Strategies such as bond ladders or Treasury Inflation-Protected Securities (TIPS) ladders can help mitigate some of these risks by creating more predictable income streams within an investment portfolio. It is also important to consider the complexity of a strategy. As retirees age, managing intricate investment and withdrawal strategies becomes harder, particularly as cognitive abilities decline.

The Role of Insurance in Retirement

Insurance products such as income annuities address some of these risks directly. By pooling longevity risk, they allow retirees to spend at levels aligned with average life expectancy instead of planning for the longest possible horizon. Those who live longer than average are supported by those who pass away earlier, through what are known as mortality credits. This risk-sharing provides income that retirees cannot outlive, which offers security that investments alone cannot match.

Insurance solutions also create behavioral and lifestyle benefits. Many retirees spend too cautiously for fear of depleting their savings. Guaranteed income can encourage more confident spending, reducing financial anxiety. For couples, annuities can simplify the household's finances if one spouse is less experienced with managing money. They also reduce the burden of decision-making later in life when managing investments may become more difficult.

Still, insurance is not without its limitations. Annuities generally lack upside growth potential, and inflation-adjusted options are available but less common and more expensive. Liquidity can also be limited, although some contracts offer partial access to funds at an additional cost. It is essential to note that all guarantees are contingent upon the claims-paying ability of the issuing insurer, and protections vary by state. For these reasons, many retirees find that partial annuitization, where insurance covers essential expenses and investments cover discretionary goals, strikes the right balance.

Finding the Right Mix.

The reality is that no single approach works for everyone. Some retirees are comfortable riding out market cycles and trusting in long-term returns, while others feel more at ease with the stability of contractual guarantees. Many discover that combining both investments and insurance creates the most effective strategy.

The right retirement income plan is less about choosing sides and more about tailoring a mix that reflects your goals, tolerance for risk, and lifestyle priorities. By carefully weighing the trade-offs and considering how each tool addresses the key risks of retirement, you can build a plan that supports your needs and gives you the confidence to enjoy the years ahead.

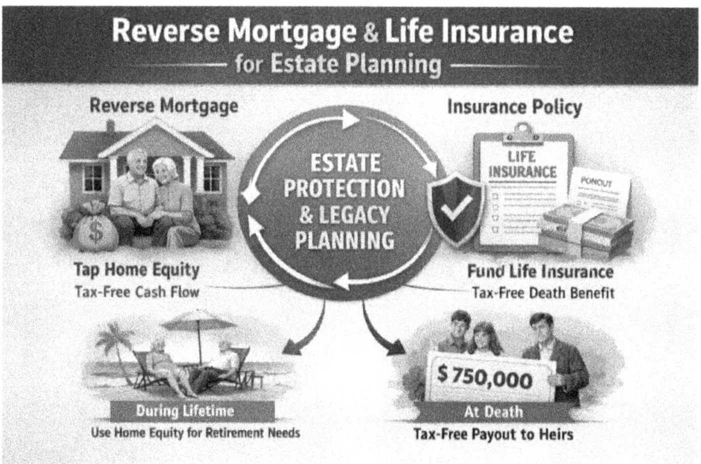

Giving Your Heirs Money Now Rather Than Later

Traditionally, we think about the legacy we leave our heirs and how it can help them after we are gone. It is nice that they can expect to inherit something, but many people are now reconsidering what it means to leave a legacy and when.

Bill Gates, Founder of Microsoft, plans to give away most of his money while he is still alive so he can see where it is going, what impact it will have, and make any adjustments accordingly.

First, let's just state that no one is entitled to your money but you, so maybe you are not concerned about leaving a cash inheritance. That is perfectly OK. Anything you decide to leave to your heirs is a gift, not a mandatory obligation.

Sometimes the better use of an inheritance is not later on after you pass, but right now. It is not written in stone that they must wait until you die to receive any money from your estate. There are times when your heirs are better off having access to some of their inheritance when it will have more of an impact on their lives for decades to come. The advantage of having funds to pay off debt, start a business, set up college funds, or help out during a financially difficult time will set them up for greater success later, and that could yield a much higher payout throughout their lives than what you would have left them.

If they have a lot of debt from a student loan or a business they started, the money they are spending to pay off that debt is money they are not contributing towards their savings. Maybe the lack of cash prevents them from paying down other debts, like high-interest-rate credit cards, a home loan, a student loan they co-signed for their kids, or any number of other reasons we get into debt.

Maybe giving them $50,000 or $100,000 now will provide a major financial benefit that compounds significantly over the years. If successful, they may be able to pay you back!

Using the funds from a reverse mortgage will allow you to contribute to their financial well-being now and in the future, without draining your savings or having to worry about living with less.

If you have multiple heirs, you will need to make sure that the others are treated fairly if you give a portion of your estate to any one individual right away and still want to give something to others later. A good attorney can help you with that.

What is important is that you don't give away the retirement savings that you need to live off of to help out others. Give them a portion of what you were planning to leave them anyway, and do it at the time they need it. Any reasonable person would appreciate the gesture, and in the end, you are leaving the decision to them about whether or not they want the money now.

As long as you clearly communicate the terms of the gift/loan and you have it in writing so everyone else is protected, you are being both generous and responsible.

Maybe you want to leave the money for your grandkids and set something up that they will remember you by long after you have left their lives.

Using the funds from a reverse mortgage, you can open up 529 accounts, or custodial accounts like Uniform Gifts to Minors Act (UGMA) or Uniform Transfer to Minors Act (UTMA). You want to discuss these options with a financial professional, as they all have pros and cons.

529 accounts allow you to open an account for a minor to save for educational expenses. The earlier you do this and the more you contribute to the account, the more likely they will have a significantly larger amount to draw from when they reach the age of 18 and go to a higher education program. It isn't just for college. You can use these funds for trade schools or any qualified education program.

Other benefits of these accounts are that they grow tax-free, and distributions are also tax-free. Also, if they don't use all the funds in the 529 plan, then you can transfer up to $35K into a Roth IRA for the plan beneficiary. Now your legacy may be helping to set up a retirement fund for them!

UGAM and UTMA accounts are savings accounts, not specific to anything like the 529 accounts are for education.

A couple of years ago, I did this loan, and I wish I had a grandma like this lady. She had one daughter with two small grandkids and wanted to leave the kids something. She had two homes and gave her daughter one for her and the kids, so the daughter was all set. She thought about opening a 529 plan to pay for the kids' college, but we discussed something she liked even more.

She took out a line of credit reverse mortgage of $185K. Then the plan was to open a custodial savings account, she decided on a UTMA, for each kid. She starts each fund with $15K and plans to add another $15K at the beginning of each year for 6 years. This way, she was under the allowed annual gift tax amount each year at that time, without triggering a taxable event. The total she gifted each grandchild was $90K. Then she planned to stop funding the accounts as she would be close to exhausting the funds she initially received.

If she follows through with that and the average rate of return is 10%, after 50 years, each child will have about $18 million in each account! She only contributed $90K, and each grandchild is estimated to have $18 million when they are about 60 years old.

Accounting for an average of 2.5% inflation, the purchasing power of that $18 million will be equal to about $4.5 million in today's dollars.

The daughter gets the 2nd home right away, and any funds left after the mom passes go toward the grandkids being pretty much set for life already, even if they don't save another penny for their own retirement.

Now, that's a really nice legacy to leave behind!

The takeaway from all this is you don't need to wait to make a positive impact on the lives of your loved ones if that is what you want to do. As long as you are comfortable with the amount you have to live off of or you have enough in reserves after you take care of others, then you have the option to make that difference now.

Generational wealth doesn't happen by accident—it happens through careful planning and smart decisions.

A Reverse Mortgage and utilizing your housing wealth can be a solution for families who want to grow wealth reliably across generations.

Good communication, setting expectations, and professional guidance can give your heirs a better future starting today.

Reverse Mortgage Line of Credit

The reverse mortgage line of credit (LOC) rate of growth may be the best feature of this program, as there are no monthly payments. The HECM is the only reverse mortgage that offers this lifetime rate of growth at a very attractive rate. As of the time of this writing, it was around 6.5%, and that growth is tax-free, and the proceeds are tax-free.

Again, the proceeds you take are not considered income, so the money has no effect on your tax rate or the amount you receive in federal benefits.

Available funds in the LOC grow over time, increasing the borrowing power for future needs. This is the power of compounding growth. The growth rate is a variable rate tied to the 10-Year Treasury yield to determine the expansion rate. This rate influences how much is available in the credit line over time.

There is no fixed payment schedule, but you can make payments if you want, on your own terms. You can change these terms as often as you need to, and any money you pay back from the funds you borrowed will automatically be credited to the same amount in the LOC. So, if you borrow $100 and you pay back that $100, then the amount you have in the LOC increases by $100.

There is no set time to withdraw the funds. They are available for as long as you meet the terms and conditions of the loan, no matter how long you live. You withdraw what you want, when you want, if ever at all.

The LOC acts as a financial safety net, supporting retirees' changing cash flow needs.

The following demonstrates how the LOC grows. The chart starts with a 65-year-old borrower and a LOC starting amount of $150,419. The rate of growth in this example is projected to average 6.63% annually.

You will see that at age 75, after 10 years, the amount in the LOC more than doubles to $306,071. After 20 years, at age 85, it grows to $622,79, and after 30 years it is estimated to be $1,267,259.

	Year	Growth Rate	LOC
0	2026	6.63	$ 150,419.00
1	2027	6.63	$ 161,493.00
2	2028	6.63	$ 173,383.00
3	2029	6.63	$ 186,148.00
4	2030	6.63	$ 199,853.00
5	2031	6.63	$ 214,567.00
6	2032	6.63	$ 230,364.00
7	2033	6.63	$ 247,324.00
8	2034	6.63	$ 265,533.00
9	2035	6.63	$ 285,082.00
10	2036	6.63	$ 306,071.00
11	2037	6.63	$ 328,605.00
12	2038	6.63	$ 352,798.00
13	2039	6.63	$ 378,773.00
14	2040	6.63	$ 406,659.00
15	2041	6.63	$ 436,599.00
16	2042	6.63	$ 468,743.00
17	2043	6.63	$ 503,253.00
18	2044	6.63	$ 540,304.00
19	2045	6.63	$ 580,083.00
20	2046	6.63	$ 622,791.00
21	2047	6.63	$ 668,643.00
22	2048	6.63	$ 717,871.00
23	2049	6.63	$ 770,723.00
24	2050	6.63	$ 827,466.00
25	2051	6.63	$ 888,387.00
26	2052	6.63	$ 953,793.00
27	2053	6.63	$ 1,024,015.00
28	2054	6.63	$ 1,099,406.00
29	2055	6.63	$ 1,180,348.00
30	2056	6.63	$ 1,267,249.00
31	2057	6.63	$ 1,360,549.00
32	2058	6.63	$ 1,460,717.00
33	2059	6.63	$ 1,568,260.00
34	2060	6.63	$ 1,683,721.00
35	2061	6.63	$ 1,807,682.00
	Total:		**$ 1,807,682.00**

Keep in mind this is a credit line, not a savings account, so any money you don't use is eliminated, and the remaining home equity belongs to the estate when you pass away or vacate the home.

This is powerful, as you can see, you have much more borrowing power later on than what you started with, so if the need arises, you can access your LOC to offset any shortfalls in your savings. Whether you use the funds because you need to or want to does not matter; this offers you the flexibility to live in retirement comfortably and affords you the option of doing things you otherwise might not be able to afford.

Now, let's have a scenario where you do decide to take the money. In this case, let's say that after 20 years, when you are 85 years old, you need to start taking an extra $3,000 a month to help you or a family member out financially, or because you are still healthy and just want to have more fun.

That $3,000 a month is $36,000 a year. Let's say you do that for five years, and due to inflation, you increase that to $4,000 a month or $48,000 a year for the next five years.

At this point, you are 95 years old! Now, let's say you increase the monthly amount to $8,000 a month to help pay for some home healthcare and other expenses. That is $96,000 a year.

In this example, you would have taken $996,000 when you reached age 100, and you would still have $233,303 left over that is available in your LOC!

	Year	Growth Rate	Other Disbursement	Accum Disbursement	LOC
0	2026	6.63	$ -	$ -	$150,419.00
1	2027	6.63	$ -	$ -	$161,493.00
2	2028	6.63	$ -	$ -	$173,383.00
3	2029	6.63	$ -	$ -	$186,148.00
4	2030	6.63	$ -	$ -	$199,853.00
5	2031	6.63	$ -	$ -	$214,567.00
6	2032	6.63	$ -	$ -	$230,364.00
7	2033	6.63	$ -	$ -	$247,324.00
8	2034	6.63	$ -	$ -	$265,533.00
9	2035	6.63	$ -	$ -	$285,082.00
10	2036	6.63	$ -	$ -	$306,071.00
11	2037	6.63	$ -	$ -	$328,605.00
12	2038	6.63	$ -	$ -	$352,798.00
13	2039	6.63	$ -	$ -	$378,773.00
14	2040	6.63	$ -	$ -	$406,659.00
15	2041	6.63	$ -	$ -	$436,599.00
16	2042	6.63	$ -	$ -	$468,743.00
17	2043	6.63	$ -	$ -	$503,253.00
18	2044	6.63	$ -	$ -	$540,304.00
19	2045	6.63	$ -	$ -	$580,083.00
20	2046	6.63	$ 36,000.00	$ 36,000.00	$586,701.00
21	2047	6.63	$ 36,000.00	$ 72,000.00	$593,993.00
22	2048	6.63	$ 36,000.00	$ 108,000.00	$601,724.00
23	2049	6.63	$ 36,000.00	$ 144,000.00	$610,025.00
24	2050	6.63	$ 36,000.00	$ 180,000.00	$618,937.00
25	2051	6.63	$ 48,000.00	$ 228,000.00	$616,506.00
26	2052	6.63	$ 48,000.00	$ 276,000.00	$613,895.00
27	2053	6.63	$ 48,000.00	$ 324,000.00	$611,092.00
28	2054	6.63	$ 48,000.00	$ 372,000.00	$608,083.00
29	2055	6.63	$ 48,000.00	$ 420,000.00	$604,852.00
30	2056	6.63	$ 96,000.00	$ 516,000.00	$553,383.00
31	2057	6.63	$ 96,000.00	$ 612,000.00	$498,125.00
32	2058	6.63	$ 96,000.00	$ 708,000.00	$438,799.00
33	2059	6.63	$ 96,000.00	$ 804,000.00	$375,105.00
34	2060	6.63	$ 96,000.00	$ 900,000.00	$306,721.00
35	2061	6.63	$ 96,000.00	$ 996,000.00	$233,303.00
	Total:		$ 996,000.00		$233,303

No other loan will offer you anything close to that, let alone without any monthly payments.

This is why the HECM is so powerful as a retirement tool. If you have that longevity, you are financially better prepared to handle it and the expenses associated with living that long.

Not only does it benefit you, but it also takes away most or all of the financial strain it may put on your family, so they can better prepare for their own retirement. You are not just doing this for yourself; in a way, it is part of your legacy. One of the best ways to take care of your kids in the future is by making sure they don't have to financially take care of you now.

Let's look at the same strategy but with the LOC starting at $200,031, only $50,000 more than our first example. Taking the same amount of money each month at the same time as before, you can see that there is much more left available in the LOC at 100 years old, $829,521. Not that you would need that much at that time, but it shows you how much more you could have taken each month, and sooner, if you had wanted to.

	Year	Interest Rate	Other Disbursement	Accum Disbursement	LOC
0	2026	6.63	0	0	200,031
1	2027	6.63	0	0	214,758
2	2028	6.63	0	0	230,569
3	2029	6.63	0	0	247,544
4	2030	6.63	0	0	265,769
5	2031	6.63	0	0	285,336
6	2032	6.63	0	0	306,344
7	2033	6.63	0	0	328,898
8	2034	6.63	0	0	353,112
9	2035	6.63	0	0	379,110
10	2036	6.63	0	0	407,021
11	2037	6.63	0	0	436,987
12	2038	6.63	0	0	469,160
13	2039	6.63	0	0	503,701
14	2040	6.63	0	0	540,785
15	2041	6.63	0	0	580,600
16	2042	6.63	0	0	623,345
17	2043	6.63	0	0	669,238
18	2044	6.63	0	0	718,510
19	2045	6.63	0	0	771,409
20	2046	6.63	36,000	36,000	792,203
21	2047	6.63	36,000	72,000	814,527
22	2048	6.63	36,000	108,000	838,490
23	2049	6.63	36,000	144,000	864,229
24	2050	6.63	36,000	180,000	891,856
25	2051	6.63	48,000	228,000	909,518
26	2052	6.63	48,000	276,000	928,480
27	2053	6.63	48,000	324,000	948,837
28	2054	6.63	48,000	372,000	970,694
29	2055	6.63	48,000	420,000	994,160
30	2056	6.63	96,000	516,000	971,353
31	2057	6.63	96,000	612,000	946,868
32	2058	6.63	96,000	708,000	920,579
33	2059	6.63	96,000	804,000	892,356
34	2060	6.63	96,000	900,000	862,054
35	2061	6.63	96,000	996,000	829,521
	Total:		$ 996,000.00		$829,521.00

You can also incorporate the LOC and your savings in a correlation strategy with the performance of the stock market. This involves you and your financial professional being more proactive in monitoring the returns on your savings and in timing when funds from the line of credit need to be withdrawn.

With this strategy, you withdraw money from your savings when the stock market performs well, but when you have a down year, you withdraw from your LOC instead.

Before we do this, we must talk about a concept called the Sequence of Returns. The phrase describes the yearly variation in an investment portfolio's performance rate of return.

The performance of your investments has a significant impact on how much you will have later on. The other factor that matters is how much cash you withdraw from the investment each year. In a down year of poor market performance, you not only lose value on the principal amount in your account, but it is made worse by taking cash out when that value is lower. This has a negative compounding effect on the performance of your investments over time.

Let's look at two different charts showing different market performances on a $500,000 portfolio. The performance on each chart is based on actual S&P 500 performance over two different 15-year periods.

In each example, we will assume that the borrower will take out $25,000 per year to help with living expenses. They do this no matter the portfolio's performance because their living expenses need to be met, and SSI is not enough to cover them.

In the first table below, we are using the S&P 500 performance from 2000 to 2015.

S&P 500 Investment Growth & Withdrawal Table (2000-2015)

- Starting Balance (Jan 1, 2000): $500,000
- **Annual Withdrawal:** $25,000 (taken at the end of the year *after* market gain/loss)

Year	Return	Gain/Loss	Value Before $25K Withdrawal	Balance After $25K Withdrawal
2000	-9.10%	-$45,500	$454,500	$429,500
2001	-11.89%	-$51,068	$378,432	$353,432
2002	-22.10%	-$78,108	$275,324	$250,324
2003	28.68%	$71,793	$322,117	$297,117
2004	10.88%	$32,326	$329,443	$304,443
2005	4.91%	$14,948	$319,391	$294,391

2006	15.79%	$46,484	$340,875	$315,875
2007	5.49%	$17,342	$333,217	$308,217
2008	-37.00%	-$114,040	$194,177	$169,177
2009	26.46%	$44,764	$238,941	$213,941
2010	15.06%	$32,219	$246,160	$221,160
2011	2.11%	$4,666	$225,826	$200,826
2012	16.00%	$32,132	$232,958	$207,958
2013	32.39%	$67,356	$275,314	$250,314
2014	13.69%	$34,268	$284,582	$259,582
2015	1.38%	$3,582	$263,164	$238,164

As you can see, after 15 years, the amount you have remaining in your portfolio would have been $238,164. If you started this at age 65 and now you are 80 years old, that is not a lot left to live off of if you live another 10-15 years. You will likely run out of money due to inflation and increased healthcare costs.

Now we will look at the performance of the S&P 500 during a different 15-year period. This time we will use the years 2010 to 2025.

We are using the same $500,000 starting balance and taking the same $25,000 annual withdrawal as before. The ending balance amount in the portfolio is very different because the performance of the S&P 500 during this time period was much better.

S&P 500 Investment Growth & Withdrawal Table (2010–2025)

- Starting Balance (Jan 1, 2000): $500,000
- **Annual Withdrawal:** $25,000 (taken at the end of the year *after* market gain/loss)

Year	Return	Growth/Loss	Value Before $25K Withdrawal	Ending Balance After $25k Withdrawal
2010	15.06%	+$75,300	$575,300	$550,300
2011	2.11%	+$11,611	$561,911	$536,911
2012	16.00%	+$85,906	$622,817	$597,817
2013	32.39%	+$193,632	$791,449	$766,449
2014	13.69%	+$104,927	$871,376	$846,376
2015	1.38%	+$11,680	$858,056	$833,056
2016	11.96%	+$99,634	$932,690	$907,690
2017	21.83%	+$198,148	$1,105,838	$1,080,838

2018	-4.38%	-$47,341	$1,033,497	$1,008,497
2019	31.49%	+$317,576	$1,326,073	$1,301,073
2020	18.40%	+$239,397	$1,540,470	$1,515,470
2021	28.71%	+$435,081	$1,950,551	$1,925,551
2022	-18.11%	-$348,617	$1,576,934	$1,551,934
2023	26.29%	+$407,994	$1,959,928	$1,934,928
2024	11.30%*	+$218,647	$2,153,575	$2,128,575
2025	16.00%*	+$340,572	$2,469,147	$2,444,147

The same $500,000 that, in our first example, was worth only $238,164 after 15 years is now worth $2,444,147 after a different 15-year period. This is a huge difference. You will now have over $2.2 million more available in your retirement portfolio than in the first example.

This is the power of the Sequence of Returns. It can mean the difference between outliving your savings or having more than enough for the rest of your life, no matter how long you live.

These examples do not take into account you taking more out of your account due to inflation, and you needing more cash later in life, or paying for healthcare or any emergencies that come up. So, more than likely, the $25,000 you take annually will increase over time and draw down your savings at an accelerated rate.

The reverse mortgage line of credit acts like a safety net for your retirement portfolio if future Sequences of Returns are not favorable to you.

Let's show this with a 67-year-old retired couple with a total savings of $900,000. They decide to take $50,000 a year from their savings, plus they increase that each year by 3.5% to account for inflation. They have a couple of options on how they want to use the reverse mortgage with their savings.

The first one is to deplete all their savings first, then use the LOC as a last resort if needed. The second option is to correlate the LOC withdrawals with the savings withdrawals, depending on how the stock market performs.

The second option takes into account the Sequence of Returns.

Let's look at both of these, and you can see the difference between them in how that affects your overall savings.

In the first example, using the LOC as a last resort, the couple exhausts all their savings by age 84, then starts using the funds from the LOC.

You can see there are some down years in their portfolio performance. Four years later, at age 87, they would have taken over $335,000 from the LOC and had nothing left in their savings.

This is fine if it meets your needs, but it puts you in jeopardy of longevity if you live a lot longer and need more cash.

Age	Year	Portfolio Change	Portfolio Beginning Balance	+/-	Annual Draw increased 3.5% yearly	End Balance after Annual Draw	Reverse Line of Credit
67	2002	-23.37%	$ 900,000	$ (210,330)	$ 50,000	$ 639,670	$ -
68	2003	26.38%	$ 639,670	$ 168,745	$ 51,750	$ 756,665	$ -
69	2004	8.99%	$ 756,665	$ 68,024	$ 53,561	$ 771,128	$ -
70	2005	3.00%	$ 771,128	$ 23,134	$ 55,436	$ 738,826	$ -
71	2006	13.62%	$ 738,826	$ 100,628	$ 57,376	$ 782,078	$ -
72	2007	3.53%	$ 782,078	$ 27,607	$ 59,384	$ 750,301	$ -
73	2008	-38.49%	$ 750,301	$ (288,791)	$ 61,463	$ 400,047	$ -
74	2009	23.45%	$ 400,047	$ 93,811	$ 63,614	$ 430,244	$ -
75	2010	12.78%	$ 430,244	$ 54,985	$ 65,840	$ 419,389	$ -
76	2011	0.00%	$ 419,389	$ -	$ 68,145	$ 351,244	$ -
77	2012	13.41%	$ 351,244	$ 47,102	$ 70,530	$ 327,816	$ -
78	2013	29.60%	$ 327,816	$ 97,034	$ 72,998	$ 351,851	$ -
79	2014	11.39%	$ 351,851	$ 40,076	$ 75,553	$ 316,374	$ -
80	2015	-0.73%	$ 316,374	$ (2,310)	$ 78,198	$ 235,866	$ -
81	2016	9.54%	$ 235,866	$ 22,502	$ 80,935	$ 177,433	$ -
82	2017	19.42%	$ 177,433	$ 34,458	$ 83,767	$ 128,123	$ -
83	2018	-6.24%	$ 128,123	$ (7,995)	$ 86,699	$ 33,429	$ -
84	2019	28.88%	$ 33,429	$ 9,654	$ 43,084	$ -	**$ 46,651**
85	2020	16.26%	$ -	$ -	$ -	$ -	**$ 92,874**
86	2021	26.89%	$ -	$ -	$ -	$ -	**$ 96,125**
87	2022	-19.44%	$ -	$ -	$ -	$ -	**$ 99,489**
						Total	**$ 335,139**

Looking at the correlation strategy shows an even better picture. This is where you get more portfolio and longevity protection. With the correlation strategy, you evaluate your portfolio performance at the end of each year (Sequence of Returns). If the portfolio value is positive, then you keep taking the draw from your portfolio; if it is negative, then take next year's draw from the LOC.

Using the same market performance chart as before, you can see now that at age 87, the savings portfolio will still have over $505,739 remaining, and the amount you took from the LOC is $356,562. The bad performing years are in red, and following those years, you take the money from the LOC.

This means you can still draw from both in future years, and you can leave that $505,739 portfolio savings to your heirs if you both have passed away at 87.

Age	Year	Portfolio Change	Portfolio Beginning Balance	+/-	Annual Draw increased 3.5% yearly	End Balance after Annual Draw	Draw from Reverse Line of Credit
67	2002	-23.37%	$ 900,000	$ (210,330)	$ 50,000	$ 639,670	$ -
68	2003	26.38%	$ 639,670	$ 168,745	$ -	$ 808,415	**$ 51,750**
69	2004	8.99%	$ 808,415	$ 72,677	$ 53,561	$ 827,530	$ -
70	2005	3.00%	$ 827,530	$ 24,826	$ 55,436	$ 796,920	$ -
71	2006	13.62%	$ 796,920	$ 108,541	$ 57,376	$ 848,085	$ -
72	2007	3.53%	$ 848,085	$ 29,937	$ 59,384	$ 818,638	$ -
73	2008	-38.49%	$ 818,638	$ (315,094)	$ 61,463	$ 442,081	$ -
74	2009	23.45%	$ 442,081	$ 103,668	$ -	$ 545,749	**$ 63,614**
75	2010	12.78%	$ 545,749	$ 69,747	$ 65,840	$ 549,656	$ -
76	2011	0.00%	$ 549,656	$ -	$ 68,145	$ 481,511	$ -
77	2012	13.41%	$ 481,511	$ 64,571	$ -	$ 546,081	**$ 70,530**
78	2013	29.60%	$ 546,081	$ 161,640	$ 72,998	$ 634,723	$
79	2014	11.39%	$ 634,723	$ 72,295	$ 75,553	$ 631,464	$ -
80	2015	-0.73%	$ 631,464	$ (4,610)	$ 78,198	$ 548,657	$ -
81	2016	9.54%	$ 548,657	$ 52,342	$ -	$ 600,999	**$ 80,935**
82	2017	19.42%	$ 600,999	$ 116,714	$ 83,767	$ 633,945	$ -
83	2018	-6.24%	$ 633,945	$ (39,558)	$ 86,699	$ 507,688	$ -
84	2019	28.88%	$ 507,688	$ 146,620	$ -	$ 654,308	**$ 89,734**
85	2020	16.26%	$ 654,308	$ 106,391	$ 92,874	$ 667,824	$ -
86	2021	26.89%	$ 667,824	$ 179,578	$ 96,125	$ 751,277	$ -
87	2022	-19.44%	$ 751,277	$ (146,048)	$ 99,489	$ 505,739	$ -
						Total	**$ 356,562**

FINRA regulates financial professionals, and they no longer view reverse mortgages as a last resort. Your financial professional has a responsibility to discuss all available options to you, and using reverse mortgages and utilizing home equity falls into that discussion. There is significant academic research that supports homeowners using their equity to help sustain a robust retirement, and the examples above demonstrate this.

When a Reverse Mortgage is Not Appropriate.

There are times when a reverse mortgage is a great solution and other times when it is not. Your home equity can be a life-changing resource, but in the wrong hands, it can be a nightmare.

This is your money, and one of the reasons the government got involved with the loan and offers so many protections is to prevent you from being taken advantage of. Seniors are a protected class, and the government tries to do what it can to make sure they are safe from predatory businesses and unscrupulous individuals who will try to take their life savings or their home.

As much as I hate to say it, the largest group of people who take advantage of seniors is your immediate family members.

Elder abuse and financial exploitation of seniors is most commonly perpetrated by people closest to them, including family members, caregivers, and trusted friends. While strangers, such as scammers, also frequently target older adults, the majority of abusers are known to the victim, often exploiting their position of trust or taking advantage of the victim's isolation, cognitive decline, or limited technical skills.

This means that the ones you love and trust are the very people who are trying to take your money more often than not. If a family member is pressuring you for money and desperately pushing you to get the loan, that is a major red flag, and you should never feel any pressure to do this.

Bill collectors, salespeople making unsolicited offers that sound too good to be true, and supposed government agencies asking for money over the phone are all common scams directed towards seniors, and if you are not sure, a phone call to the police might be warranted.

Any outside influence you feel is directing you to get any loan or buy any product or service you don't need or want is unethical.

If you have a history of poor money management, then maybe you can have an accountant or have someone you trust handle the reverse mortgage proceeds for you. If you know you don't have the discipline to manage money well, then hold off on getting the reverse mortgage until you have someone who can do it on your behalf. If you have a diagnosis of some dementia that you know will get progressively worse, then this is really prudent as you are protecting you from your future self when your memory and good judgement become impaired and are no longer reliable.

6.

Using a Reverse Mortgage to Purchase a Home.

Most people are unaware that you can use a reverse mortgage to purchase a home. This feature was added in 2009. This is important because in 2025, 36% of all homes purchased in the U.S were by people 65 and older.

Why would you consider a reverse mortgage to purchase a home versus a traditional loan?

The most obvious reason is because you will not have any monthly payments ever. Also, with many retirees living on a fixed income, they may not qualify for enough of a loan to buy the home they want.

There is also the issue of your credit score. If it is low because you don't use a lot of credit in retirement, you may have a difficult time qualifying for a loan at all. A reverse mortgage is not credit score-based.

Many retirees find that the house they raised their family in is now too much to maintain, or they want to move away to be closer to family and friends, or for lifestyle reasons.

There are four distinct reasons you may consider buying a home with a reverse mortgage.

1. Having access to more funds means you can afford the home you really want in the area you want to live in and not settle for less. This is convenient if you are moving to a more expensive area to be closer to family and friends, or to a destination where you want to retire, like a master-planned community with many amenities, near a beach, a mountain resort, or for some other lifestyle decision.

2. You can afford monthly payments for now, but want the option to stop in case something comes up later, or one of you passes away, and the other lives there on a reduced income. Payments are not required, but if you want to, you can create any payment schedule you want and change it as needed.

3. You don't want to make any payments at all.

4. You want to pocket the money you saved that would have been locked up in your home. This way, the amount of cash you keep can grow, so you build up your retirement savings.

Let's look at an example of how a reverse mortgage for purchase can work.

A couple that is both 70 years old decides they want to move closer to one of their children and grandchildren in another state.

They have $450,000 from the sale of their home, but the new homes they are looking at are closer to $500,000.

They borrowed $200,000 from the reverse mortgage to help purchase the home they decided on. This benefits them because now they are in the home they truly wanted and didn't need to settle for less.

They can take the $200,000 from the reverse mortgage and only $300,000 in cash from the $450,000 they got for their old home, then buy the new home. That means they have $150,000 left over ($450,000 in cash they had minus $300,000 they applied toward the new home equals $150,000 left over).

Now they take the $150,000 they saved and put it back into their retirement account. Not only do they have the extra $150,000, but they also have any interest that accumulates on that amount year after year. This second benefit means they have more available for them in retirement.

Here is another scenario.

Often, the homeowner has not sold their current home yet, and they are not ready to move into the new home because they don't have enough cash, and they don't want monthly mortgage payments, so a traditional loan is out.

With the HECM for Purchase, they can withdraw funds from the reverse mortgage and possibly add them to their retirement savings to purchase the new home right away. Then, when the original home sells, they can replenish the funds they took out of their savings.

This can get tricky because they may have to pay taxes or penalties on funds they withdraw from a retirement account, depending on the type of account. If this is the case, then this is not a good option, but if they don't have any penalties or taxes owed on the money they withdraw, then it could make more sense.

This can be a good option to get the sale closed on the new home sooner, so you don’t lose the opportunity to buy it, rather than waiting a long time for the original home to sell, and, while that happens, the new home is sold to someone else. It is something you most certainly want to consult your accountant or financial professional about before you make any decision.

There are approval conditions for a reverse mortgage for purchase, like any reverse mortgage. You would need to consult your reverse mortgage loan officer first to determine how much you qualify for, before looking for a home, so you know what funds will be available to you.

7.

Proprietary Reverse Mortgages

Proprietary reverse mortgages work similarly to the FHA-insured HECM but have some differences as well. These reverse mortgages are products that are specific to the lender that created them, and they can be offered by other lenders or brokers who are authorized to sell them. There are no monthly payments, and the loan does not get paid back until the last borrower passes away or vacates the home. Same as the HECM.

They have origination fees and third-party fees like the HECM, but no Initial Mortgage Insurance Premium (IMIP) because that is a fee exclusively for the HECM.

They charge higher interest rates than HECM loans because there is no IMIP. This means the lender assumes all the risk of getting paid back.

One of the biggest differences with the proprietary reverse mortgages is that their home value maximums are much higher than those of the HECM. As of 2026, the HECM max home value for a single-family home is $1,249,125. Values above this amount are not recognized, so for more affluent areas where home values are higher, they may want to look at the proprietary loans if they need more money. Most proprietary reverse mortgages have no home-value limit, but as of now, their lending limit is around $4 million.

There are pros and cons to these proprietary loans.

The higher interest rate means that the home equity is reduced at a much faster rate. If keeping as much home equity as possible to pass on to your heirs is a concern, then this may not be the right solution for you.

If you have a need or desire to extract as much of the home equity out of your home as possible and are not worried about the remaining equity when you pass away, then this should not be an issue.

Some states only offer these products at a fixed rate, so depending on where you live, you may be required to take all the available cash at closing since fixed-rate reverse mortgages do not offer a line of credit.

This forces you to take more cash right away than you need and at a high interest rate. If you do not take all the cash at closing, then you permanently lose the amount you didn't take.

So, let's say you have $800,000 total available to you. If you decide to only take $500,000 at closing, you lose the $300,000 you didn't take.

If taking the maximum amount at closing is desirable, then again, this should not be a concern. The good thing is you can take all the available cash you are entitled to, so unlike the HECM, the amount you get with the fixed rate is not significantly less than the variable rate loan.

Even if you can get a line of credit, the line of credit on proprietary reverse mortgages is only offered for a maximum of 10 years. After that, you would need to refinance the loan, and with the higher interest rates reducing equity at an accelerated rate, there is a high possibility that the loan balance may be too high to be refinanced by then.

Since the home values are higher, this means the origination fee can also be higher. The HECM origination fee is maxed out at $6,000, but a proprietary origination fee can be tens of thousands of dollars if the home value is high enough. Like the HECM, these fees are rolled into the loan, so you are not paying them out of pocket.

If you live in a non-HUD-approved condo, the proprietary reverse mortgage can be a better option for you since the HECM can only be used with HUD-approved condos. The qualifications for eligibility are different for each lender, and not all lenders are approved in all states, so you are limited to which options are available.

There are many different proprietary reverse mortgages, and each one will offer different loan amounts, different interest rates, and terms & conditions, and the qualifications for loan approval, such as credit score and income, will vary for each lender.

There are times when, even though your home value can justify using a proprietary loan, the HECM may still be a better option.

Sometimes you may be better off starting with the HECM reverse mortgage and later on, switch over to a proprietary reverse mortgage. The reason is that you will preserve more equity in your home at the lower HECM rate than if you started taking cash at the higher proprietary interest rate. Let's look at an example of this.

In this example, we are looking at a borrower with a $3 million home, and with a HECM, they qualify for only $500,000 since the maximum home value can only be $1,249,125.

With a proprietary reverse mortgage, they can get $1.2 million, significantly more.

The interest rate on the HECM loan is around 6%, but with the proprietary loan, it is around 8.5%.

If the borrower does not need all the cash right away, then they can start with the HECM. Even though it offers a lower amount of cash, it is at a lower interest rate.

When they deplete all the $500,000 (plus the increased amount due to the rate of growth in the line of credit during that time) from the HECM at the lower rate, they can then refinance the loan into a proprietary reverse mortgage and access much more cash at the higher interest rate.

The borrower is taking the first $500,000, plus the amount from the rate of growth, at the lower 6% rate, and then taking the rest of the money offered by the proprietary loan at the higher 8.5% rate. This strategy preserves more equity in the home to leave for your heirs or for you if you sell it later on.

Also, the home value may have increased over time, so when the borrower refinances the loan, an increased home value would offer more cash from the proprietary loan.

8.

Historic Concerns About Reverse Mortgages

The Reverse Mortgage Question: If Reverse Mortgages Are So Good... Why Doesn't Everyone Get One?

If housing wealth can provide a guaranteed income—and can help protect retirees from outliving their money—why don't more people voluntarily get the loan? On paper, a reverse mortgage solves some of retirement's biggest problems:

You live longer than expected, so you need more cash than previous generations of retirees. Markets underperform at the wrong time, and you withdraw your savings faster than anticipated.

Your money runs out before you do, and you are forced to either sell your home or take some other action you didn't plan for.

And yet...most people still avoid using housing wealth.

So, what's going on?

It isn't that reverse mortgages are bad. It's that human beings don't make retirement decisions like spreadsheets. We make them like humans. And when you look closely, the reasons people hesitate are actually very rational.

1) Fear of Regret

Even "safe money" buyers carry a hidden fear. "What if I take the money... and regret it?" Not because the loan is risky—but because commitment feels risky. This is loss aversion in action. People would rather keep flexibility, even if it costs them long-term security.

2) Lack of control

A lot of people don't mind having the money. They mind feeling locked into the loan. Even if the reverse mortgage is objectively strong, the emotional reaction isn't.

3) Complexity

Most people can't explain a reverse mortgage. And when people can't explain something, they assume it's designed to trick them or benefit the lender, not the homeowner. That doesn't mean reverse mortgages are shady. It means complexity creates a trust gap.

4) Lack of trust in non-bank lending institutions.

People trust banks. They trust their 401(k) website.

But a lender they had never heard of? Even strong ones? A lot of consumers worry about "What if the company fails?" Even when you explain the loan in detail and all of the built-in regulated protections... the emotional concern still lingers.

5) Fear of disinheriting heirs.

This is a big one. Many retirees don't want to "spend" their heir's inheritance. They want to preserve it, so they resist anything that sounds like:

"If I die, the lender keeps my home." Even though reverse mortgages offer heirs rights & protections, this is still a big concern. They can also offset this fear with existing or new insurance policies. The fear persists because it's not a math problem. It's a legacy problem.

6) Underestimating longevity risk.

This is the quietest and most dangerous part of retirement planning. Most people underestimate how long retirement really is. Retirement isn't 10–15 years anymore. For many couples, it's 25–35 years, which is almost as long as they had been saving for retirement.

Which means retirement isn't just a "nest egg" problem... It's an income problem. People don't use housing wealth and reverse mortgages because they're bad. People avoid them because they don't want to feel like they're making an irreversible decision.

7) Reverse Mortgage Costs.

One of the most common concerns with reverse mortgages is the costs. It is true that the initial costs are higher than most any other loan, but when you consider the benefits you get, the costs become much more attractive than the fees of other options.

Financial Advisors- You typically pay them 1% or more of assets under management (AUM) annually, even if you lose money in the market. If you have $500K in AUM, then you are paying at least $5K annually for as long as the assets are being managed. If that is 20 years, then you paid out $100K regardless of performance. The reverse mortgage fees are a fraction of that.

Selling your home- Selling is a tough decision because you need to decide where you will live after the sale. You are paying a realtor around 5%-6% commission plus the costs of moving on a $500K home, which is around $25K-$30K in commissions plus around another $3K-$5K in moving costs. And you still need to consider the decorating costs associated with moving into a new home and possible storage costs related to the move.

Benefits You Pay For- Part of the fees of the reverse mortgage go to the fact that you are not required to make any monthly payments. This gives you flexibility in deciding if you want to pay down any loan balance or pay yourself the money and put the savings in your retirement fund. Think about it. You can pay the mortgage company, or you can pay yourself. No other loan offers you that choice. You are also getting an option to open a line of credit that will always grow tax-free, no matter what happens in the housing or stock market. You are insured by the FHA, so that all the money will always be available even if the lender goes bankrupt. Even the banks limit you to an FDIC maximum of only $250K per account. Brokerage accounts are insured up to $500K. The reverse mortgage insurance has no limit.

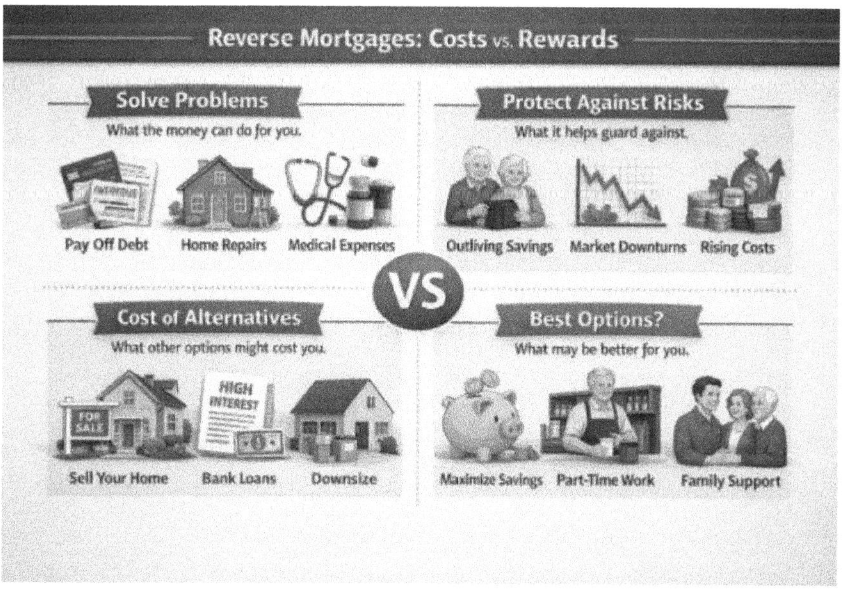

So, looking at the fees, you need to ask yourself:

1. What problems can the money help me with?
2. What risks am I being protected from with this loan?
3. Are the expenses really that much compared to other options?
4. What else can I do and at what costs?

When you compare the reverse mortgage costs to the benefits you receive, you are getting a great value!

8) Is it really a good investment?

For a single male earning an average wage every year and who retired in 2020 at age 65, lifetime Social Security and Medicare benefits would equal about $640,000, while total lifetime taxes paid into SS would be just shy of $470,000. This means that you are expected to receive roughly a total of 36% more than what you paid into SS. This is assuming SS is able to pay out 100% of the benefits you are entitled to, and right now it is projected to start paying only 80% of that amount in 2033.

On a $400K mortgage and a 5% interest rate, you will be paying about $773K over 30 years. Of course, you will get back some of that via taxes from the interest you paid on. If you access some of your home equity and open a $150K line of credit, over a 30-year period, you will have received close to $1 million. You don't even need to wait 30 years to start taking the money. If you can start taking it at 15 or 20 years, you will still receive more money than what you paid into Social Security while you were working.

The reverse mortgage line of credit uses the equity you built up in your home to pay out a benefit that is more than what SSI is expected to pay you over a typical life span, and it is tax-free.

You paid into SS, and the return on those payments is small compared to the money you paid into your home and the amount of money you can get back with the reverse mortgage line of credit.

I don’t think I ever heard anyone say, "I don’t want Social Security income or Medicare, even though I paid for it." Why would you not consider using the home equity that you also paid for?

In uncertain times, stability becomes a strategy. With retirement planning needing to stretch 30 years or more, you can count on uncertainty to pop up during that timeframe.

Access to a growing tax-free line of credit provides exactly that—a secure, cash-flow-driven asset that compounds into long-term family wealth.

If you’re looking to build financial security for your retirement, a legacy for your children and grandchildren, this is an option worth exploring.

Are Reverse Mortgages Safe? In the beginning, these products lacked protection for borrowers, spouses, and heirs, which is why they received so much negative word of mouth. Over the decades, the government has implemented regulations to address these concerns and strengthen consumer protections.

Reverse Mortgage Counseling.

Before submitting a reverse application, borrowers must meet with an independent, HUD-approved third-party counselor, either by phone or in person. Reverse Counseling is an impartial educational resource to help seniors and their family members make an informed decision about reverse mortgages. The process is mandatory for all reverse mortgage transactions.

Non-Recourse Protection.

This is a non-recourse loan. This means even if home values decrease, the borrower or their heirs can never be liable for any amount over the value of the home. No one will ever go into debt, and all your other assets are protected.

Mortgage Insurance.

Guarantees non-recourse protection and ensures borrowers will receive loan payments as agreed upon by the loan terms, regardless of prevailing home values.

Interest Rate Adjustment Caps.

For loans with an adjustable interest rate, there is a limit on how much the rates can change over the life of the loan. In most cases, it is 5% over the start.

Non-Borrowing Spouse Protections.

To be eligible for a reverse mortgage, only one borrower must be over the age of 62 (except for the state of Texas, where both spouses need to be at least 62). Furthermore, eligible non-borrowing spouses can remain in the home without making monthly payments even if the borrowing spouse moves to assisted living or passes away.

Monthly Payments Are Optional.

A common misconception about reverse mortgages is that monthly payments are not allowed. In fact, the borrower can choose to make a payment at any time.

No Prepayment Penalty.

The loan can be repaid at any time without penalty. The borrower is also free to refinance a reverse mortgage.

9) My Financial professional does not discuss them or doesn't know enough about them.

Traditionally in the U.S., financial professionals are not trained about reverse mortgages because you need a special license to offer them, and Financial Advisors, Accountants and Certified Financial Planners don't have this license. Also, when reverse mortgages first came out, FINRA guidelines only recommended that reverse mortgages be used only as a last resort. Even the financial community did not like these loans- at first.

Once additional protections were established, FINRA revised its guidance so that reverse mortgages can now be part of a comprehensive retirement strategy. The issue now with their lack of knowledge is that most of the brokers' training has not caught up to this new guidance. Hence, the financial professionals still lack the proper education to know how to integrate the loan into retirement planning. They need to consult a reverse mortgage specialist like me to help them do that.

Financial professionals rarely like to discuss subjects they are not very comfortable with because clients ask further questions about them. If they can't answer them, they come across as either incompetent or biased against that product. Either way, they want to protect their reputation, so many do not want to discuss things that jeopardize that reputation with their clients.

I offer many training opportunities to the financial professional community, and when we discuss specific scenarios so they can see how their clients benefit from the loan, they more often than not come around and realize how much it improves their clients' retirement outcome. They can't ignore the math, and neither should you.

9.

Common Objections.

"My Kids Will Help Me Financially." Maybe, but historically, unlikely.

It is fantastic that you have a child or two that will step in to help you financially in retirement, but is it really always the best choice for you and them?

Let's say you need an extra $1,000 a month right now to make ends meet. Accounting for inflation, that increases in 5 years to $1,500 a month.

Over 10 years, that will be $150,000. That is $150,000 that your children could have applied toward their own retirement savings and 10 years of gains on that money they missed out on.

This doesn't take into account the money they would probably need to contribute towards any home repairs or routine upkeep of the home, and any health care costs that arise.

With a reverse mortgage line of credit, you could have withdrawn that same amount, and they would be able to better finance their own retirement or their grandkids' college savings with the money they saved.

Also, what happens if they lose a job, have a health issue that requires them to be on short-term or long-term disability, or they run into some other situation that stresses them financially? They will likely need to stop contributing to your monthly allowance, and you will be left financially stuck. Asking someone to help you financially month after month, year after year, for a decade or two and having them do it consistently is asking a lot.

In reality, money almost always flows from the parents to the kids; seldom is it the other way. This is because of all the expenses associated with raising a family and saving for the grandkid's college and for your own kid's retirement. Even if they truly want to help, almost always, something happens that pauses the payments at some point, and you are stuck as to what to do at that time.

If only one child contributes the money, and when you pass the home goes to multiple children, will the others repay the one who contributed the $150,000 to you, or will that child be out that money permanently? This will cause a lot of tension between siblings.

The reverse mortgage line of credit avoids all these issues and gives you the security and peace of mind that the monthly income will

always be available, no matter what happens in life with you or your family.

HECM for Purchase Objection.

"I don't want to contribute a large portion of my retirement funds to purchase the home so I will take out a traditional mortgage. I want the funds to remain in my retirement account and grow, and I can afford the monthly payments."

Dr. Wade Pfau addressed this scenario in his book "Reverse Mortgages: How to Use Reverse Mortgages to Secure Your

Retirement". In the book, he addressed this using a $450K purchase price and offering three scenarios.

1. Pay cash for the home.
2. Open a 15-year fixed-rate traditional mortgage with 20% down.
3. Use the HECM for purchase to cover as much of the home cost as allowed and pay the remainder in cash.

"Using the HECM for Purchase strategy to fund a portion of the home's purchase price provides a larger net legacy than paying cash for the home in 75 percent of the historical cases. On average, the HECM for Purchase increases the net real legacy value of assets by $121,301," stated Dr. Pfau.

In addition, the HECM for Purchase strategy provides a larger net legacy than taking out a 15-year traditional mortgage in 69 percent of the historical cases. Though this percentage is slightly less, the average net real legacy value was $161,340 more when using the HECM for Purchase strategy.

Also Dr. Pfau noted from his analysis, "in general, the HECM for Purchase strategy provides a viable option for those thinking about moving more permanently into an eligible home during their retirement. By funding a portion of the home purchase through the HECM, the investment portfolio maintains more assets at the start of retirement. This lowers the withdrawal rate from the investment portfolio needed to cover spending, setting it on a course for greater long-term sustainability and growth. Even after accounting for the costs of the reverse mortgage, retirees are mostly left in a better position by using home equity in this coordinated manner."

If they only receive SSI and have very little in savings, they really benefit much more from using the H4P. When they sell their original home, they can take some of that money and keep it to boost their savings. Having a mortgage payment while only having SSI is waiting for a default to happen when something else comes up they need cash for, or they wind up living off their credit cards, and that almost always ends in disaster.

Getting the Line of Credit Only When You Run Out of Other Options.

Getting a reverse mortgage line of credit should be done as soon as you are eligible!

Too often, people only consider the reverse mortgage after they have exhausted all other sources of funds available to them. This is the worst time to get the loan.

Integrating your home equity into your comprehensive retirement strategy as soon as possible gives you much more available funds in retirement, since the line of credit amount grows each year. It uses the power of compounding tax-free growth, so the amount you start with can be worth many times more later in life.

This allows you to develop a coordinated strategy to maximize spending all your assets in a much more sustainable method and improve the longevity of all your financial resources.

You Don't Own Your Home

A reverse mortgage is a lien on your property, like any other mortgage.

Your heirs get to inherit the home (or whoever you leave it to). When the last borrower passes, the heirs will have to pay back whatever the balance is due, either by refinancing the mortgage or, if they want, selling the home. They keep the remaining equity after the balance is paid off.

If at any time, you decide you no longer want to live in the home, then you can sell it, pay off the balance due, and keep the remaining equity from the sale.

Since there are no monthly payments you are obligated to pay, you do not risk getting foreclosed on due to being late or having no payments. You still need to pay your property taxes and homeowner's insurance (HOI), but that is part of homeownership, whether you have a reverse mortgage or not.

The foreclosure process takes years. If you cannot afford the property taxes, HOI, HOA dues, and upkeep of the home with a reverse mortgage, then you would have struggled even more financially if you didn't have the reverse mortgage.

They Are Too Expensive.

Compared to what? If you start with $200K and 20 years later, it grows to $800K, then the costs of getting a reverse mortgage are much less than what you would pay a financial advisor over the same 20 years if you were paying them 1% of assets under management in an S&P ETF fund for the same returns.

If you sell your home, then you are paying a realtor around 5%-6% in commission and moving costs, and those fees are also much higher than the fees associated with a reverse mortgage.

If you open a traditional line of credit, it will never grow; in fact, the bank can reduce or eliminate it if they want to. This can never happen with a reverse mortgage, as the government ensures the money will always be available. Part of the fees with the reverse mortgage is that the government guarantees the money will always be available and the growth of the line of credit. The fee is an insurance policy for those guarantees.

Do we even need to discuss living off credit cards? You want to go into debt with a 25% interest rate or higher? Nothing will ruin your finances faster than credit debt. It spirals out of control faster than most people realize, and should be used only in retirement as a last resort. Credit cards and medical debt are the two biggest reasons for seniors filing for bankruptcy.

When you consider the costs of other options and the money that you get in return, the fees are very reasonable.

Here is another exercise for you to try. You have read all about the reverse mortgage and what it does. Knowing what you do now, try to list the pros & cons of why you would or would not get the reverse mortgage. Look at your lifestyle, things you are able to do, and what you either would like to do more of or can't do at all now.

Are you happy with your current situation, or would a reverse mortgage help you feel more fulfilled in retirement? What other options do you have, and would they make you happier or not?

Are you comfortable with the current savings you have to last the rest of your life, and is there enough in case any emergencies come up for either you or a family member?

PROS Yes for the reverse mortgage	CONS- No for the reverse mortgage

10.
Conclusion

Remember these words from the beginning of the book?“Every life is organized around a small number of events that either propel us or bring us to a grinding halt. We spend the years between these episodes benefiting or suffering from their consequences until the arrival of the next forceful moment.

A person’s worth is established by the number of these defining circumstances we are able to create for ourselves.”

If you are wondering if it is too late at 65, 75, or 85 years old to create another defining circumstance that can change your life, the answer is no; you are not too late for that to happen.You are still in charge of your life and future, and you have more to say about how that looks than anyone else. If you think you want to change your retirement, I showed that you still have the resources, options, and opportunities to do this.

A reverse mortgage can be more than a last-resort option. When used strategically, it can serve as a financial bridge, allowing retirees to delay Social Security and potentially increase their lifetime income.

For the right homeowner, this approach can improve cash flow flexibility, protect investments, and strengthen long-term retirement security. But it requires careful analysis and a clear understanding of the costs and obligations.

Reverse mortgages have evolved significantly over the decades. Even FINRA, which used to recommend them as loans of last resort, has changed its stance and now suggests that a reverse mortgage can be part of a broader retirement income plan when used carefully.

Most of you have heard of these loans, but were never prepared to discuss them or know how to incorporate the proceeds into a comprehensive retirement strategy.

I have two questions for my readers:

1. What percentage of you would say you are 100% certain you currently have all the funds you need to live the retirement you want?
2. If you could be offered a guaranteed resource you already have that would always increase your cash flow, preserve retirement assets, and protect you from market volatility, wouldn't you want to know about it?

The untapped equity in your home is your largest non-performing asset. You can turn that equity into a safe, reliable performing asset that will provide higher income for you or act as a type of insurance policy that will help prolong your asset's longevity. This will create better outcomes for them by preventing their retirement funds from running out.

If you don't believe me, then I challenge you to contact me and go over the numbers so you can see first-hand the benefits of using housing wealth in retirement planning. Once you see the benefits, you won't be able to unsee them!

Retirement is a new lifestyle. Money is the tool that maintains that lifestyle. The more money you have and the more secure that cash is, the greater your enjoyment and peace of mind will be. Use all your assets: home equity, your savings, insurance, annuities, and most of all, your intelligence to know that integrating all of your resources will lead to a better retirement outcome for you.

I've talked about how everyone approaches retirement income differently and alluded to how these differences suggest different ways of building your retirement plan.

Retirement is often painted as a picture of freedom: long mornings with coffee and no alarm clock, spontaneous travel, time to read, relax, and finally catch up on the things you never had time for. And while all that sounds great, the reality of retirement is a little more nuanced. Once the novelty wears off, many retirees find themselves asking a bigger question: now what?

While most people spend years preparing financially for retirement, fewer take the time to plan for what daily life will actually look like once work is no longer part of the picture. That lack of preparation can leave retirees vulnerable to some tough emotional challenges. Feelings of loneliness, boredom, and even depression aren't unusual, especially when the structure, identity, and purpose that a career once provided suddenly disappear. It could also potentially strain relationships with loved ones as everyone adjusts to schedules and routines without the framework of a full-time job. Couples who were used to saying goodbye in the morning and "how was your day?" in the evening are now suddenly together in the middle of the day as well.

Intentionally planning for the emotional and psychological side of retirement can lead to better outcomes for retirees once they transition away from full-time work. This involves thinking about what brings you fulfillment, how you might stay engaged, and who you might socialize with. Incorporating these elements into your planning can make all the difference. Preparation for a meaningful retirement starts with asking the right questions. What makes you feel energized? What gives you a sense of purpose? How do you want to spend your time, and who do you want to spend it with? These aren't always easy questions, but they're essential for creating a fulfilling retirement experience.

Planning for the emotional side of retirement might not feel as urgent as crunching the numbers, but it can be just as important. A retirement filled with purpose, passion, and connection isn't something you stumble into; it's something you create. So take the time to visualize your future. Not just where you'll live or how you'll budget, but how you'll fill your days with meaning. Because retirement isn't the end of the story, it's the start of a brand-new one. And the best stories are written with intention.

Good retirement planning blends clear financial analysis with personal preferences, risk tolerance, and real-world trade-offs.

If you have ever felt unsure about how to evaluate competing retirement options, maybe taking a comprehensive look at all your options is required.

Leaving home equity on the table when it can make the difference between a comfortable retirement or a challenging one, is a missed opportunity with lifelong consequences.Women, as a group, still earn roughly 83 cents for every dollar made by men. This limits their ability to save for retirement and reduces their future Social Security benefits. While women actually make up almost 55% of people 62 and older receiving Social Security benefits, the average payment for women is about 21% less than for men.

Compounding the problem, women are less likely to invest than men, in part because of lower confidence about how to engage with the stock market, according to a 2024 survey by SoFi. And since women tend to outlive men by about five years, they'll need their Social Security and retirement savings to go further. "Women have less to save with and longer to live, so a reverse mortgage benefits them more than men.

Football Analogy

You can look at your entire retirement portfolio like a football game.

You are the owner of your team, and “Life” is the other team you are trying to beat. Your head coach is your financial advisor. The financial advisor’s job is to make sure you win by having more points (dollars) than the other team has points (expenses) at the end of the game.

The assets that pay you are your offense team as you want them to score as many points (dollars) as possible. These would be your savings and the money from the reverse mortgage.

The defense tries to prevent the other team from scoring their points (increased expenses). The less points they have (again, dollars) the better your odds of winning.

The defense’s job is to try and reduce the risk of them scoring. In your retirement this would be represented by bonds, CDs, your insurance or annuities policies. They all act as a hedge against risks.

You coordinate your team’s assets so that you can score the most points while not having to rely on some risky plays that could jeopardize the game's outcome. A proper defensive strategy mitigates the possibility of risk that "Life" throws at you to defeat you.

You can't win a game on offense or defense alone. They must work together to ensure a better outcome.

This means using all available resources you have. The more resources you have access to, the more likely you will win this game!

Finally, what does a happy retirement look like for most people? Many studies have been done to answer this, but here are the most common findings, and see if you agree with them. It is also to remind you what retirement could be like and to be honest with yourself and ask if you are living that retirement now or can maintain it for the rest of your life.

Healthcare Access

Adequate access to healthcare has been shown to increase life expectancy by approximately two to five years for both men and women aged 65 and older.

This is especially important in urban and rural areas, highlighting the critical role of healthcare access in seniors' overall health, quality of life, and longevity.

While this isn't directly linked to retirement happiness, it's probably safe to equate increased life expectancy and quality of life with optimism and a positive frame of mind.

Family Connections

Research published on the National Library of Medicine website shows that seniors who live with family members report better social integration, well-being, and happiness than those living alone.

Additionally, other studies have found that seniors with supportive family relationships experience higher levels of happiness, as family ties provide emotional support, caregiving, and a sense of belonging.

Financial Security

Being free from financial worries and having the means to enjoy a productive retirement won't surprise anyone in terms of retirement happiness.

People who control their finances are calmer and happier. They are also much less likely to worry about finances like pensions and healthcare insurance.

Conversely, evidence suggests that worrying about pensions or stressing about running out of retirement funds prematurely can have an adverse effect on happiness levels.

Active Social Relationships

It sounds cliché, but everyone needs someone. Human beings are social creatures. Finding and maintaining social relationships generally becomes more complicated the older you get.

There is quite a bit of research suggesting that enjoying a healthy social life—and having the financial security to do so—directly affects happiness levels.

Moreover, strong family ties, friendships, and a sense of belonging within a community improve life satisfaction and reduce loneliness. Seniors with active social lives report higher levels of retirement happiness, mainly because they have emotional support and a sense of purpose in life.

Volunteering

Research performed by the Royal Voluntary Service in England revealed that 64% of retirees who volunteer to help others and support good causes report being happier.

Anyone who has ever helped someone else will testify that it delivers enormous satisfaction. This, coupled with the sense of purpose and social element of volunteer work, makes retirees happier and more positive.

Physical Health and Activity

It might surprise you that 42% of people aged 55 and over are physically inactive, compared with 29% of the total population. Yet 10 minutes of physical activity per week or just a little exercise per day has the potential to boost happiness levels.

What's more, Frontiers in Psychology presumes there's a strong and direct link between regular physical activity and the notion of well-being. What's the key takeaway here? Well, it could be that more exercise typically leads to increased happiness and self-esteem.

Experiential Living

Experiential living is a life focused on actively engaging in different activities and experiences. This can mean different things to different people. For some, it's socializing and nothing more. For others, it involves pushing boundaries by parachuting from planes or driving sports cars around race tracks.

According to one study, retirement is directly linked to "experiential well-being." Forty percent of that well-being was attributed to having more time to seek out new experiences.

Mental Stimulation

Exactly what stimulates the mind of a senior is a subjective matter. For some, it might involve completing word puzzles or quizzes. For others, it might mean managing a local group or running charitable events. Whatever mental stimulation looks like, evidence suggests it improves cognitive function.

According to a study by the NIH, cognitive stimulation significantly improves cognition. The results indicated a standardized mean difference of 0.40, indicating a moderate improvement in cognitive performance after engaging in mental activities like puzzles or learning new skills.

If you can push your brain power to its limits regularly, there's evidence that your efforts might make you a little happier.

Activities that challenge the brain – such as learning new skills – are linked to improved happiness. Keeping the mind engaged contributes to a more fulfilling and enjoyable life while also helping to slow cognitive decline.

Freedom and Independence

Autonomy and control are aspects of life most people take for granted. However, when you reach a certain age, the inevitable consequences of the aging process can take a toll on the capabilities you never imagined could go away. For some people, those consequences necessitate care and supervision – both of which interfere with a senior's freedom and independence.

Research shows that, in many cases, seniors who can maintain their independence are happier than those from other age groups. Around 76% of 65- to 74-year-olds report feeling generally happy – compared with just 51% of 25- to 34-year-olds. As long as seniors are free to live on their terms, they appear to be among the happiest people in the world.

Pets

Did you know that around half the seniors in the U.S. own at least one pet? That may be down to the emotional and physical benefits of close contact with domestic animals.

From those daily walks to constant companionship, studies have shown that owning pets supports increased fitness levels, reduced stress, and enhanced mental well-being, especially in regard to the debilitating effects of loneliness that retirees may face. Many seniors express how their pets influence their retirement planning decisions, including where to live.

Happiness in Retirement Begins with Good Health

If you're not healthy – or constantly worried about what might happen if you require healthcare service – you can't hope to be truly happy in retirement.

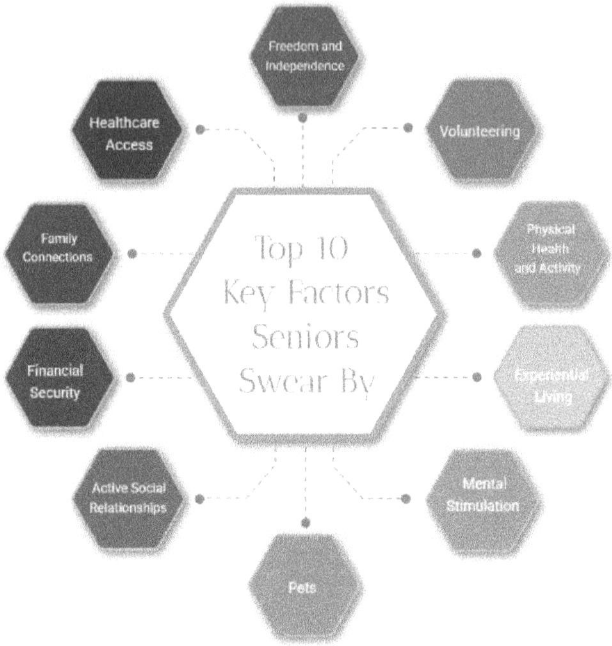

Thank you and I wish you the best retirement you could ever hope for!

www.ingramcontent.com/pod-product-compliance
Lightning Source LLC
LaVergne TN
LVHW050916210926
848482LV00012B/455